PSYCHOLOGY OF DANCE

Jim Taylor, PhD
Ceci Taylor, MA, MA

Human Kinetics

Library of Congress Cataloging-in-Publication Data

Taylor, Jim, 1958-
    Psychology of dance / Jim Taylor, Ceci Taylor.
      p. cm.
    Includes bibliographical references and index.
    ISBN 0-87322-486-8 (pbk.)
      1. Dance—Psychological aspects.   2. Dancers—Psychology.
    I. Taylor, Ceci, 1929-   . II. Title.
    GV1588.5.T39   1995
    792.8'01—dc20   94-40398
                                                    CIP

ISBN: 0-87322-486-8

Acquisitions Editor: Judy Patterson Wright, PhD
Developmental Editors: Ann Brodsky, Lori K. Garrett, Anne Mischakoff Heiles
Assistant Editors: Kirby Mittelmeier, Susan Moore, Dawn Roselund, and John Wentworth
Copyeditor: Rebecca Tavernini
Proofreader: Karin Leszczynski
Indexer: Joan Griffitts
Typesetter and Layout Artist: Impressions, a Division of Edwards Brothers, Inc.
Text Designer: Judy Henderson
Cover Designer: Jack Davis
Photographer (cover): Karla G. Nicholson (Aspen, CO)
Photographers (interior): DanceAspen and School of the Hartford Ballet
Illustrator: Tara Welsch
Printer: Versa Press

Human Kinetics Books are available at special discounts for bulk purchase. Special editions or book excerpts can also be created to specification. For details, contact the Special Sales Manager at Human Kinetics.

Printed in the United States of America   10   9   8   7   6   5   4   3

Human Kinetics
Web site: http://www.humankinetics.com/

United States: Human Kinetics, P.O. Box 5076, Champaign, IL 61825-5076
1-800-747-4457
e-mail: humank@hkusa.com

Canada: Human Kinetics, 475 Devonshire Road, Unit 100, Windsor, ON N8Y 2L5
1-800-465-7301 (in Canada only)
e-mail: humank@hkcanada.com

Europe: Human Kinetics, P.O. Box IW14, Leeds LS16 6TR, United Kingdom
(44) 1132 781708
e-mail: humank@hkeurope.com

Australia: Human Kinetics, 57A Price Avenue, Lower Mitcham, South Australia 5062
(088) 277 1555
e-mail: humank@hkaustralia.com

New Zealand: Human Kinetics, P.O. Box 105-231, Auckland 1
(09) 523 3462
e-mail: humank@hknewz.com

Table of Contents

Preface

Dance has historically relied on tradition-bound methods of preparing dancers. Many dance teachers, however, have come to realize that traditional methods of dance education do not fully prepare students for the demands of a career in dance. Traditional training also does not always result in dancers reaching their full artistic potential. Dance teachers find themselves asking

- why do some of my students lack confidence in their dancing?
- how can I teach students to overcome stage fright?
- how can I motivate my students to work their hardest?
- how can I help my dancers fully recover from injury?

With the significant advances in exercise science and psychology, and the increase in the level of sophistication and professionalism among dance teachers, clear and practical information about psychological issues applied directly to dance teaching is now needed.

We wrote this book to provide you with an understanding of the psychological issues that most influence dance performance. In *Psychology of Dance* you will find understandable information about important issues related to mental preparation for dance. In addition to theoretical and background information, there are simple, practical techniques that you can incorporate into your own teaching to optimize your dancers' performance. Moreover, *Psychology of Dance* is designed for instructors at all levels, in all styles of dance. Whether you teach in a dance school, university, or a professional dance company, whether you teach ballet, jazz, modern, or another form of dance, and whether you teach beginners or professionals, this book should be beneficial. It can also help dancers, psychologists, therapists, and counselors who work with dancers.

Psychology of Dance is intended to assist dance teachers in developing the *Performing Attitude* in their dancers. We define the *Performing Attitude* as the quest for and attainment of the highest degree of personal and artistic fulfillment from participation in dance. The performing attitude comes from developing critical psychological areas, including motivation, self-confidence, intensity, and concentration.

The impetus to write *Psychology of Dance* came from several directions. In his work with sport coaches and athletes, Dr. Jim Taylor found the response to these techniques very positive. In her 40 years as a professional dancer, professor of dance, and counselor to young and professional dancers, Ceci Taylor witnessed the profound need for a more sophisticated understanding of the psychological aspects of dance instruction. In the past several years, we have written a series of articles about the psychology of dance published in *Dance Teacher Now* and have noted our readers' interest in a more comprehensive look at the psychology of dance performance.

Psychology of Dance fills a void of information in this area. It integrates the latest scholarly information related to performance, presenting it in a reader-friendly format. It provides you with knowledge, techniques, and exercises to directly and positively impact the psychological influences on your dancers' performances by addressing such concerns as motivating dancers, assessing and developing self-confidence, helping dancers to control their level of intensity and concentration, using imagery skills, and understanding the role that psychology plays in the treatment and rehabilitation of dance injury. You will learn how to pull together this information to design and implement a *Psychological Program for Enhanced Performance* that complements your traditional dance training regimen to help dancers perform their very best. With this knowledge, you can accomplish three essential goals: helping your dancers reach their fullest artistic potential, ensuring that the dance experience is fun and fulfilling, and creating an environment that fosters personal and professional enrichment. In other words, you can assist them in developing the *Performing Attitude.*

Acknowledgments

I would like to thank the thousands of performers and instructors in dance and sports with whom I have worked over the past decade. What I learned I learned from them.

Most importantly, I would like to express my appreciation and love to my co-author (who happens to be my mother), for without her collaboration, this book, my first, would not have been possible.

J.T.

To all my students and teachers who taught me about dance.

To my husband and children who taught me about life.

C.T.

Special thanks to Shel Taylor for his time, energy, and insight in reviewing the manuscript.

J.T., C.T.

Raising the Curtain
on the Performing Attitude

The teacher stands at the crossroads of the dancer's world, holding one rein on creativity, one rein on technique, one rein on aesthetics, one rein on the living process, one rein on the future, one rein on the past. All these reins strain at once as, with the skill of a Roman charioteer, the teacher maneuvers this thundering energy toward a goal (Louis, 1977, p. 84).

Dress Rehearsal:
Mutual Understanding Between Instructor and Dancers

Charlene is a new student at your school. In her audition she shows considerable potential, although her skills are not refined. To assimilate her quickly into the school's training philosophy and to tailor future training to her needs, you want her to learn as much as possible about the dance training you offer and you want to learn about her in every aspect of her dance.

1. What are the critical aspects of your dance philosophy and training regimen that she should know?
2. What are the most important areas you must learn about her in order to facilitate her development?
3. How can you both best obtain this information about each other?
4. How can Charlene and you know whether your perceptions of what she needs to focus on match?
5. How can you use this information to establish an essential rapport and build trust so that you can work together effectively?

You spend many hours each week working with your dancers on their physical and technical development. Like other instructors and dancers, you may consider mental preparation as important or more important than physical and technical training. Yet like most instructors and dancers, you actually devote little time to the impact of psychological issues on dance performance. Like traditional dance training, the quest for the *performing attitude* is long and arduous. You would not expect dancers to increase their strength and flexibility from physical training once a week or their technique by working on it for a few hours. The only way to improve in any area—whether physical, technical, artistic, or mental—is through commitment, hard work, and patience. Time and effort must be expended on every aspect of training, including physical, technical, and mental preparation. Fortunately, developing the performing attitude does not require long hours of practice. It can develop from information and techniques that are part of regular lesson plans. This relatively small investment in time and effort that you and your dancers make—through a psychological program for enhanced performance (PPEP)—can lead to a big return: your dancers performing the best they possibly can. That is what the performing attitude is all about.

HOW CHANGE HAPPENS: THE POSITIVE CHANGE FORMULA

A fundamental tenet of *Psychology of Dance* is that dancers must produce positive change in themselves to perform their best. Change of any sort, whether physical, technical, or mental, does not occur easily or automatically. Lasting and meaningful change requires three steps (see Figure 1). The first step is *awareness*: that is, dancers recognizing what they are currently doing and the need for change to improve their performances. This step requires assisting your dancers to understand the strengths and weaknesses in their dance.

The second step is taking active steps to *control* what they want to change. In this phase you provide them with information and skills to assist them in making changes they seek. Third, positive change becomes ingrained through *repetition*. This step requires that dancers expend the time and effort to master their positive changes. By using this three-step formula throughout training, dancers can develop the performing attitude.

PERFORMING ATTITUDE PYRAMID

In making changes to perform their best, dancers develop a sound foundation of skills that lead to the performing attitude. These skills influence each other in a particular order (see Figure 2) that we call the *performing attitude pyramid*. At the base of the pyramid is high motivation, which ensures your dancers' total preparation. Preparation leads to high self-confidence and truly believing in their ability to perform their very best. Self-confidence in turn leads to an ideal level of intensity as your dancers begin a performance. Ideal

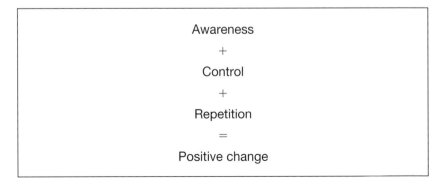

Awareness

+

Control

+

Repetition

=

Positive change

Figure 1   Positive change formula.

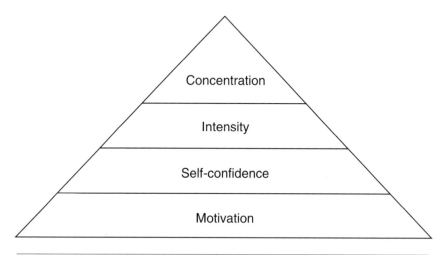

Figure 2   Performing attitude pyramid.

intensity then produces focused concentration during performance. The pyramid's apex is the development of the performing attitude and the ability to perform at the highest level.

WORKING WITH DANCERS TO DEVELOP THE PERFORMING ATTITUDE

Dancers of all ages and abilities can benefit from learning to use psychological skills. It is never too early or too late for dancers to start developing sound psychological skills. Just as dancers work on physical and technical skills at an early age to develop to a high level, they can begin to master psychological ones as well. By teaching sound thinking, emotional, and behavioral skills early in dancers' careers, you can avoid many potential difficulties. On the other hand, dance psychology is a relatively young field, so established professionals who are motivated can also benefit from an introduction to these ideas. The only true prerequisite for developing the performing attitude is a desire or commitment to perform better.

When you work with dancers to develop the performing attitude, you should consider the commitment, time, and motivation they have. Serious dancers who have high aspirations may be more willing to commit time and energy to a sophisticated, multifaceted psychological program for enhanced performance (PPEP). You may help these dancers design and implement highly structured and in-depth PPEPs that involve participation both within and outside the studio. Younger and less motivated dancers may not be willing to commit their time to so involved a program. They should not be asked to implement a PPEP outside of the studio time. Their PPEP can focus on practicing psychological skills during class time. In fact, these dancers may not even realize that they are practicing psychological skills in the studio. You can discuss with the dancers how detailed a PPEP they should have and on what areas they need to develop.

Explaining the Intangible

Unlike physical and technical skills, psychological skills are not tangible. Some dancers may tend to undervalue the importance of what cannot be seen, touched, or directly measured. Also, anything that has not been a regular part of their traditional dance training may be viewed suspiciously. They may have misconceptions about psychology, such as it being hocus-pocus or something that will just mess up their heads. As a result, you may have to convince your dancers of the importance of preparing psychologically for their performances.

Several approaches can help you educate your dancers. Well-known dancers have described the benefits of psychological preparation, and you might read their remarks or have them make presentations to your dancers. These anecdotal descriptions can make a powerful impression on young dancers. Talking with your dancers in a group setting about what enables them to dance well or causes them to dance poorly is also an effective way to provide evidence. By simply expressing their ideas about the effect of psychology on dance performance, many dancers become aware of how influential psychological factors are.

You also are a significant role model to your dancers, who often look to you to determine what is important. When they hear you talk about the value of psychological preparation and when they see you make it a regular part of dance training, dancers will begin to accept its importance.

A Learning Process

Developing the performing attitude is a learning process. It is best not to force your dancers to use these techniques, but allow them to grow naturally and gradually. It is better to start off small and increase the level of PPEP than to try to do too much too soon. An overload of information and responsibility will inhibit, rather than encourage, involvement. Instead, when the opportunity arises, point out situations where psychological issues are affecting performance. You can also incorporate simple and fun strategies into dance training without labeling them as psychological techniques.

Ideally, awareness and appreciation for psychological issues begin early in the dancers' careers. Then convincing dancers of the importance of psychological skills training is not necessary; they view it as simply another part of dance training that will enable them to perform their best. If dancers have not had this early experience, give them accurate information that is meaningful to their dancing and that allows them to make an informed decision about whether and to what extent to participate in the psychological preparation for dance.

PERFORMING ATTITUDE PROFILING

Dancers can see and feel increased strength and flexibility. They know they are improving technically by their ability to execute new skills, through feedback from instructors, and by watching themselves on video. With psychological development, however, the most tangible evidence of improvement is a vague feeling of, for example, being more confident or more relaxed.

Performance profiling, developed by R. J. Butler (1989), is a simple graphic method to overcome this obstacle. Specifically, performance profiling, or what we call *performing attitude profiling*, assists in identifying and understanding dancers' strengths and areas in need of further development. It is a visual representation of how dancers perceive themselves in relation to a variety of psychological, emotional, social, physical, and technical factors that impact dance performance. You and your dancers then can use this information to clarify and develop appropriate strategies to maintain strengths and enhance areas that need further development.

The first step in change is awareness. To benefit from performing attitude profiling, dancers must first develop a *learning attitude*, or an openness to evaluating themselves honestly and to considering the information they garner from performing attitude profiling in a positive, constructive way. All dancers, novices or professionals, can obtain information from performing attitude profiling. Beginning dancers can gain insight to facilitate their development. Experienced dancers can learn valuable information to overcome hurdles that have limited their growth and that may enable them to move up to a new level of performance. Performing attitude profiling can enable dancers to perform even better than they have by developing a broader repertoire of skills in a wider range of performance situations. Performing attitude profiling can help you more fully understand your dancers, ensure that you and your dancers agree on what they should be working on, and provide greater direction and structure to their training.

Using Performing Attitude Profiling

Have your dancers complete the Profile worksheets by rating themselves on a 1 to 10 scale for each performance factor. They should shade in each segment of the profile below the number they give themselves. What emerges is a graphic representation of how they perceive themselves on these relevant performance factors.

You may also wish to complete a profile for each of your dancers. You can then compare the two profiles and discuss any discrepancies that may exist. This provides two benefits for your dancers. First, it helps them to more accurately perceive their abilities and understand themselves. Second, it helps ensure that you and your dancers share the same perceptions, thus enabling you to work together more effectively on their development as dancers. You may copy and use these profile forms with your dancers.

Performing Attitude Factors

Through our extensive work with dancers, we have identified 12 psychological, emotional, and social factors in the Personal Profile that seem to have the greatest influence on dance performance (see Performing Attitude Personal Factors list). Performing attitude profiling may also be used to help you and your dancers identify and understand their strengths and areas in need of improvement in their physical and technical development. The Physical Profile identifies 12 physical factors critical to dance performance (see Performing Attitude Physical Factors list). Because specific technical factors vary, depending on the style of dance and the level of development, *you* should label each segment of the Technical Profile to fit the current needs of your dancers.

Understanding the performance factors provided in the three profiles can improve your work with dancers; enhance their focus and direction in training; facilitate your dancers' development mentally, physically, and technically; and ultimately maximize their performances.

Performing Attitude

Personal Factors

Confidence — How strongly you believe in your ability to dance your best in a performance. (1:not at all; 10:very much)

Motivation — Your level of your motivation to train and perform. (1:very low; 10:very high)

Intensity — How well you are able to reach and maintain ideal intensity during performances. (1:poor; 10:ideal)

Focus — How well you are able to stay focused during performances. (1:negative, distracted; 10:positive, focused)

Imagery — How often you use imagery to enhance your dance performance. (1:never; 10:often)

Understanding — How well you understand what skills you need to develop to perform your best. (1:not at all; 10:completely)

Training — How well you are able to put 100% focus and intensity into your training. (1:0%; 10:100%)

Adherence — How well you are able to adhere to your training program. (1:poorly; 10:completely)

Social support — How much social support you are receiving from instructors, other dancers, family, and friends. (1:none; 10:considerable)

Communication — How well you are able to communicate with instructors and other dancers. (1:poorly; 10:well)

Performance — How well you are able to dance during performances compared to training. (1:much worse; 10:much better)

Mental skills — How much you incorporate mental skills into your training and performances. (1:not at all; 10:a great deal)

Performing Attitude

Physical Factors

Strength — The amount of force you can generate for a specific muscle group (e.g., leaps). (1:low; 10:high)

Stamina — Ability of the muscle and cardiovascular system to keep working for a long period (e.g., a long solo). (1:low; 10:high)

Coordination — Ability to execute complex movements and combinations (e.g., multiple pirouettes). (1:poor; 10:excellent)

Timing — Ability to execute movements and combinations to the music and with others (e.g., pas de deux). (1:poor; 10:excellent)

Flexibility — Ability of muscle to lengthen (e.g., hamstring stretch). (1:poor; 10:excellent)

Agility — Ability to change direction with quickness and power (e.g., prances in all directions). (1:poor; 10:excellent)

PERFORMING ATTITUDE

PERSONAL PROFILE

Name _____   **Date** _____

Directions: Twelve personal factors that are important for the Performing Attitude are identified on the profile below. Be sure you fully understand the factors before completing the profile. Indicate how you currently perceive yourself on the 1 to 10 scale for each factor by drawing a line at that level and shading in the area *below* it. A score below a 7 indicates an area in need of further development.

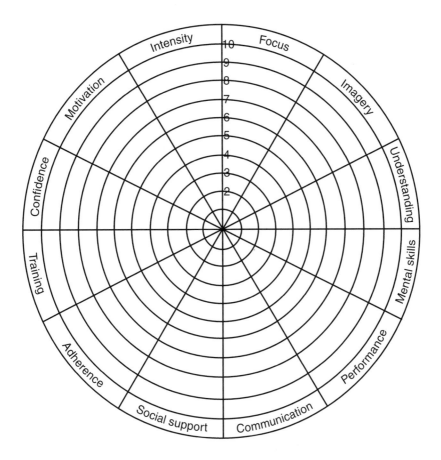

Balance — Ability to maintain center of gravity and equilibrium during a movement (e.g., en pointe). (1:poor; 10:excellent)

Pain Tolerance — Ability to endure pain and discomfort from training and injury (e.g., muscle pulls). (1:poor; 10:excellent)

Recovery — Ability to recover from intense training period (e.g., maintain high intensity, no burnout). (1:poor; 10:excellent)

Health — Degree of injury, illness, or fatigue you now have (e.g., knee injury, flu, burnout). (1:poor; 10:excellent)

Sleep — How well you are sleeping (e.g., length and quality). (1:poor; 10:excellent)

Diet — How well you eat and get sufficient nutrition (e.g., high carbohydrates, low fat, at healthy weight). (1:poor; 10:excellent)

Center Stage:
How to Use Performing Attitude Profiling

- Explain the value of performing attitude profiling to your dancers.
- Describe the performing attitude performance factors and ensure full understanding.
- Have dancers complete the personal, physical, and technical profiles.
- Complete a profile of each of your dancers or meet with them individually to discuss accuracy.
- Based on profile information, specify goals and use in developing a PPEP.
- Chart progress in the three areas by having dancers complete the profiles periodically.

PERFORMING ATTITUDE PROFILING IN ACTION: ENRIQUÉ

Enriqué, a 17-year-old dancer who recently was admitted to a prominent metropolitan ballet school, possessed tremendous potential and raw talent. He faced a great deal of work to refine and further develop his abilities. The school director, Ms. Barnes, knew that for Enriqué to get the most out of his training, his instructors and he had to identify and understand his strengths

PERFORMING ATTITUDE

PHYSICAL PROFILE

Name _____   **Date** _____

Directions: Label each section of the profile with the physical conditioning factors that are important for your dance performance. Then indicate how you currently perceive yourself on the 1 to 10 scale for each factor by drawing a line at that level and shading in the area *below* it. A score below a 7 indicates an area in need of further development.

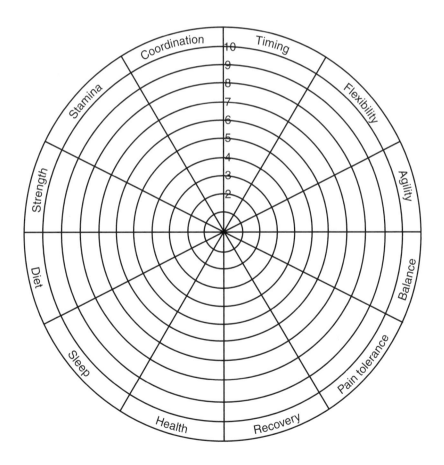

PERFORMING ATTITUDE

TECHNICAL PROFILE

Name _____   **Date** _____

Directions: Label each section of the profile with the technical skills that are important for your dance performance. Then indicate how you currently perceive yourself on the 1 to 10 scale for each factor by drawing a line at that level and shading in the area *below* it. A score below a 7 indicates an area in need of further development.

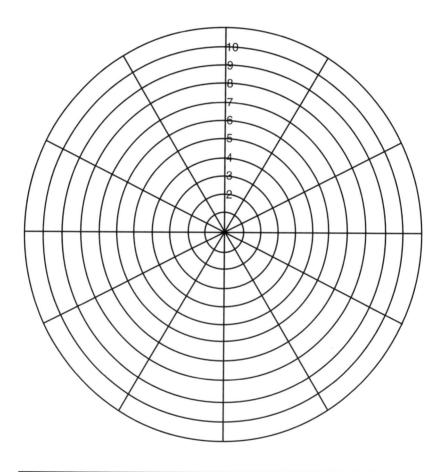

and areas in need of improvement. Ms. Barnes had also noticed that in the first few weeks of classes, Enriqué seemed somewhat uncomfortable with his principal instructor, George.

Ms. Barnes decided to use performing attitude profiling to facilitate the process. Enriqué completed the three profiles. George also filled out the profiles based on his observations of Enriqué. Then Ms. Barnes met with Enriqué and George to review the profiles. Though Enriqué has some insight into his abilities and what he needed to work on, there were some discrepancies between his perceptions and those of his teacher. After discussing these differences, they agreed on the direction Enriqué's training should take. Referring to the personal profile (see Figure 3), they identified four psychological areas Enriqué would work on: confidence, intensity, imagery, and mental skills. Then, using the physical and technical profiles (see Figures 4

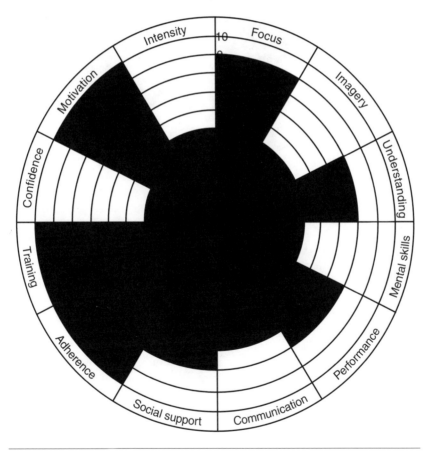

Figure 3 Enriqué's personal profile.

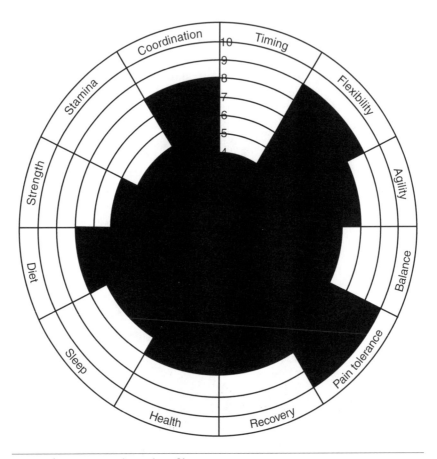

Figure 4   Enriqué's physical profile.

and 5), they detailed the areas he needed to focus on, including strength, stamina, timing, turn-out, Grand Jetés, and partnering. They specified how they would work on these areas, set goals for each area, and organized a schedule using the PPEP to allow all of the identified areas to be addressed in a structured, timely manner.

Using performing attitude profiling gave Enriqué and George focus and direction in Enriqué's future dance training. The discussion also enabled George to establish a greater rapport with Enriqué, and it allowed Enriqué to have a greater sense of trust and comfort with his instructor.

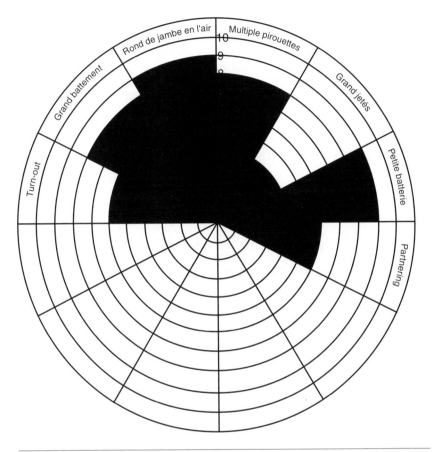

Figure 5   Enriqué's technical profile.

PERFORMING ATTITUDE PROFILING AS FEEDBACK

When they complete the profiles, you and your dancers will have a graphic description of what they perceive to be their strengths and areas for future development. Regardless of whether you complete a profile for each of your dancers, you should review their profiles with them to determine the accuracy of their perceptions. Meetings to discuss the profiles also help establish rapport and build trust in a working relationship.

You can also use performing attitude profiling to help specify objectives and the amount of time and effort that should be devoted to each goal. These profiles are useful for identifying what factors to address in the development of a psychological program for enhanced performance (see chapter 8).

Performing attitude profiling can provide you and your dancers with regular feedback on progress toward the goal. Specifically, your dancers can complete a profile about every four weeks, and the profiles can be compared to show what progress has been made. These comparisons can then be used to modify training or goals as needed. For example, a lack of progress in a certain area, as demonstrated by the profile, would indicate the need to alter the goal or change the strategy for developing the area. In contrast, if the profile shows attainment of a certain goal, it might suggest that area is adequately developed, and your attention can be turned to another area for work.

How To Use This Book

Dance teachers often wonder how to find the time to work on the mental side of dance and how they can possibly develop the expertise to help dancers with psychological preparation. The primary purpose of *Psychology of Dance* is to give you the important psychological concepts and skills related to dance performance in an understandable and practical framework.

A good first step is to familiarize yourself with the techniques by first reading this book cover-to-cover over a period of a few weeks. Make note of specific information, exercises, and ideas that can help your dancers currently. After reading the entire book, return to those important topics you noted and read them over again. Try them out on yourself and see what works best for you. This firsthand experience will help you to convince your dancers of the importance of psychological preparation and will enable you to determine the best way to teach the skills to your dancers.

Do not expect to take in and use all of the information the first time you read this book. Select two or three issues you consider important to introduce to your dancers. Next experiment with different techniques to develop the areas you have chosen. Then, using the performing attitude profiles and the PPEP, set specific goals and techniques and organize a structured plan to achieve your objectives.

Each chapter addresses central psychological issues that concern dancers. Chapter 1 looks at the importance of motivation, showing you how to maximally motivate your dancers. Chapter 2 demonstrates the essential role of self-confidence, explaining how to develop self-confidence. The third chapter describes how intensity levels affect dance. You will learn useful ways for your dancers to control their levels of intensity, enabling them to perform their best. Chapter 4 discusses concentration and how effective focus enhances training and performing. In chapter 5 you will learn how dance imagery can enhance all facets of dance. Chapter 6 concerns slumps, stress, and burnout among dancers and how dancers can learn to prevent and relieve these difficulties. Chapter 7 introduces the critical issue of injury in dance. You will see the role that psychology plays in the rehabilitation of dance injury and learn about a psychological rehabilitation program (PReP). To conclude, chapter 8 pulls together information from previous chapters into the psychological program for enhanced performance (PPEP), which describes how you and your dancers can develop a comprehensive mental training program within and outside the studio.

These chapters all follow the structure of an actual dance performance. Dress Rehearsal describes a common scenario related to the chapter's topic and asks questions about how you might handle the situation. It is a prelude that sets the stage for the information you will read in the chapter. Center Stage appears within each chapter to highlight important information and techniques. Center Stage emphasizes key points to return to when reviewing a chapter's contents. At the end of each chapter is a recap that we call Encore, which summarizes the key points in the chapter.

And now, let the dance begin.

ENCORE

- A problem with addressing psychological issues is that they are not tangible.

- Performing attitude profiling offers you and your dancers a practical means for identifying and understanding strengths and areas in need of improvement in a variety of personal, physical, and technical areas that impact dance performance.

- Your dancers must be willing to honestly evaluate themselves and view the information in a positive and constructive way.

- Performing attitude profiling can benefit dancers at all levels of ability.

- Use the profiles to specify goals and to assess progress.

1

Motivation

I intend to work for this dance of the future. I do not know whether I have the necessary qualities; I may have neither genius nor talent nor temperament. But I know that I have a Will; and will and energy sometimes prove greater than either genius or talent or temperament. (Isadora Duncan in Cohen, 1974, p. 127)

Dress Rehearsal:
Increasing Motivation

Tony is a 13-year-old ballet dancer in a small dance school. He has always been a hard worker and dreams of becoming a professional dancer. Recently, two other talented male dancers with whom Tony was friends left for a larger school. Now Tony is, by far, the best young male dancer in the school. But recently, Tony seems to have lost his motivation. He has been missing classes, and when he does attend, he does not put forth his usual full effort. Tony also no longer interacts with other dancers in the school.

1. How would you explain the decline in Tony's motivation to dance?

2. How would you motivate Tony?

Some dancers seem to have everything—strength, skill, artistry—yet do not realize their potential. Other dancers seemingly lack the requisite talent yet rise to a far higher level. Herbert Ross, director of *The Turning Point,* once said, "I was tall and didn't have the natural attributes, but I studied like a maniac" (Gelatt, 1980). What accounts for one dancer succeeding against the odds and another failing to live up to expectations? One quality that may separate these dancers is motivation. Consider dancers who have had it all: Graham, Nureyev, Baryshnikov. Twyla Tharp (1992) described this rare combination when she said,

> I also had a will that let me eliminate everything that stood in the way of my becoming the best dancer I could be. By a gradual process . . . I had invested every bit of my dreams, my hopes, my energies in defining myself as a dancer. (p. 57)

WHAT IS MOTIVATION?

Motivation, in its most basic form, involves the ability to initiate and persist at a task. Applied to dance, motivation is the capacity for dancers to persist in the face of boredom, fatigue, pain, and the desire to do other things. Motivation is so important because it is the only factor related to performance that dancers can control. As the *performance formula* in Figure 1.1 indicates, three factors contribute to the quality of a performance: motivation, ability, and task difficulty. Ability and task difficulty cannot be easily changed in a short time. However, motivation can be increased or decreased at any time.

At a more practical level, motivation means dancers putting 100% of their time, effort, energy, and focus into their preparations. Simply put, it means doing everything possible to become the best dancers they can be. "Being a dancer was an act of total commitment costing not less than everything" (Martha Graham in Stodelle, 1984, p. 59). Motivation will influence several important areas.

One area is physical conditioning, where benefits depend largely on how motivated dancers are to expend time and effort in exercise. Technical training in the studio is another area that motivation affects significantly. Mental preparation depends more heavily on motivation because it is not typically included in dance training programs. Finally, excellence in dance involves a lifestyle of commitment. Motivation influences lifestyle choices in the areas of sleep, diet, schedules, family and social relationships, and alcohol, drug, and cigarette use. "Frequently the most talented people are those most aware of their own deficiencies and most willing to work hard to overcome them" (Lee Strasberg in Penrod & Plastino, 1980, p. 40).

Motivation initiates an important progression that affects the entire preparation and performance process (see Figure 1.2). As a consequence, motivation is the starting point of the performing attitude pyramid, which becomes the foundation of the Psychological Program for Enhanced Performance (PPEP) and begins the process leading to the development of the performing attitude of dancers.

Motivation + (Ability − Task Difficulty) = Performance

Figure 1.1 Performance formula. Ability and task difficulty stay fairly constant during the course of a performance season, so the only thing dancers have control over is their motivation. Increased motivation results in expending more time and effort in physical, technical, and mental training.

High Motivation → Total Preparation → Maximum Performance

Figure 1.2 Motivation progression.

IDENTIFYING INDIVIDUAL MOTIVATION

Not all dancers are motivated by the same things. They train and perform for a variety of reasons. Some dance because they aspire to excel in the field. Others dance for social reasons—to be with their friends. Still others participate for the satisfaction of mastering the artistry of dance. All of these dancers are motivated, yet all are motivated by different things. As a result, you cannot use one generic motivational technique to motivate everyone. Rather, you must identify the motivational needs of each of your dancers and work to motivate them accordingly. For example, a class that focuses on drilling may motivate those dancers who enjoy developing skills, but may alienate those who enjoy dance as a social activity.

Identifying and satisfying the individual motivational needs of your dancers affects them at two levels. First, motivation influences *participation*. Dancers are drawn to many other attractive activities, and if they are not motivated in class, in rehearsal, and during performances, their desire to continue in dance will diminish. Second, as mentioned earlier, motivation influences *performance*. Highly motivated dancers will expend the time and effort that will result in optimal performance. As Agnes de Mille suggests, "A dancer . . . who fears or dislikes work and failure should get out immediately. It's extremely hard work and if you don't take joy in it too, if you're not excited and inspired by it, it's not for you" (Rosen, 1977, p. 10).

SYMPTOMS OF HIGH AND LOW MOTIVATION

In addition to using the Personal Profile, you can assess the motivation levels of your dancers by observing them during class and rehearsal. Your dancers will show some clear behavioral manifestations of high and low motivation.

Symptoms of High Motivation

Highly motivated dancers are characterized by a high level of energy. They are typically enthusiastic about class and rehearsal, and have a keen interest in learning new ways to improve. They are often the first dancers to arrive and the last to leave, they expend 100% effort, and they spend extra time learning new skills or rehearsing a role.

Highly motivated dancers do not like taking time off from training, they always complete all aspects of their training regimen, and they want to train even when they are ill or injured. These dancers also have specific and clearly defined goals.

Symptoms of Low Motivation

Dancers who lack motivation show little eagerness for class or rehearsal and only do the bare minimum of what is required of them, rarely expending full effort. These dancers take unneeded days off and cut short the training in which they do participate. They use minor or nonexistent injuries and illness to get out of class or rehearsal. Finally, they often have unclear, easily attainable, or unreachable goals.

Center Stage:
Increasing Motivation in Your Dancers

Have your dancers

- set macro goals,
- train with a regular partner,
- decide what dancer they aspire to be like and display his or her name or photograph where they can see it every morning,
- place motivating key words, phrases, and photographs where they can see them regularly,
- maintain a dance diary,
- use dance imagery, and
- ask themselves the two daily motivational questions.

DEVELOPING MOTIVATION

Developing and sustaining motivation in your dancers is one of the most important tasks you must accomplish. Without adequate motivation, as the motivation progression indicates, your dancers will not be properly prepared, and as a result, will not perform to their potential. You want to instill in your dancers a level of commitment like that described by Merce Cunningham (1951):

> The most essential thing in dance discipline is devotion, the steadfast and willing devotion to the labor that makes the classwork not a gymnastic hour and a half, or at the lowest level, a daily drudgery, but a devotion that allows the classroom discipline to be moments of dancing too. . . . (p. 250)

You can use a number of techniques to enhance and maintain dancers' motivation.

Setting Goals

"Never undertake great enterprises without first making a careful plan; commit your thoughts to paper; read them a hundred times over . . ." (Jean Georges Noverre in Cohen, 1974, p. 63). One of the most effective means of improving motivation in your dancers is to have them set a variety of goals toward which they can strive. Dancers often have a dream that they want to fulfill, for example, dancing for a major company, but do not know how to realize it. Goals provide the means to reach the dream. Goals are like a road map for dancers to follow to reach their destination.

Goal setting has beneficial effects on performance. First, goal setting concentrates and guides dancers' actions. Second, it drives the output of effort and perseverance. Whatever goal is set, dancers expend energy in relation to its difficulty and exert effort until the goal is attained. Third, goal setting encourages seeking new ways to enhance performance. To illustrate the value of a goal setting program for your dancers, consider the example of Martha, a 21-year-old ballerina who has been with a small metropolitan dance company for one year.

Dance Fitness Analysis.   The Dance Fitness Analysis (DFA) helps dancers identify their strengths and weaknesses that influence achieving their goals. The DFA specifies four areas of preparation critical for achieving higher order goals: physical, mental, technique, and lifestyle. By becoming aware of which areas need work, your dancers can set goals to improve them (see the Dance Fitness Analysis worksheet).

Martha completed the DFA and found that her strengths included technique and the ability to handle pressure during performances. Conversely, lack of optimal physical conditioning and poor eating habits were among her weaknesses. Identifying these problem areas enabled her to set clear training and lifestyle goals and to focus on them every day.

Macro goals.   To perform at their best, dancers need to set five types of goals. First, *long-term goals* refer to dancers' dreams; what they ultimately want to achieve during their dance careers. Martha's long-term goal was to become a leading dancer in a major ballet company. Second, *performance season goals* involve what dancers want to accomplish in the upcoming performance season. Martha wanted to become a prima ballerina in her present company and be chosen for the touring company. Third, *performance goals* indicate what dancers want to achieve in particular performances during the season. Martha's aim was to earn a leading role in at least two ballets. Fourth, *training goals* specify what dancers need to do in their physical, technical,

Dance Fitness Analysis

Directions: In the space below, indicate your strengths and weaknesses in the four areas (also use your performing attitude profiles).

Area	Strengths	Weaknesses
Physical (strength, flexibility, stamina)		
Mental (motivation, confidence, intensity, concentration)		
Technical (double turns, jumps)		
Lifestyle (sleep, diet, school, social)		

and mental training to reach their performance goals. "Progress in dance requires ceaseless effort if we are to build a solid emotional, intellectual, and technical foundation upon which to erect a superstructure of artistic achievement" (H'Doubler, 1968, p. 107). These goals are especially critical because they provide the specific means to achieve higher order goals. Martha's training goals included improving multiple turns and turn-outs. Fifth, *lifestyle goals* refer to what dancers need to do in their daily lives, including diet, studying, work, and family and social relationships. Martha needed to improve her diet and sleep habits. Achieving the training and lifestyle goals lead dancers progressively to attaining their performance and long-term goals (see the Macro Goal-Setting Program for Dancers worksheet).

Goal guidelines.   You should follow several guidelines in helping your dancers establish meaningful goals. First, *goals should be challenging but*

Macro Goal-Setting Program For Dancers

Directions: In the space below, set your long-term, performance season, and performance goals.

Long-term goals (ultimate dream):

Performance season goals (for this year):

Performance goals (for specific performances):

Directions: In the space below, set your training and lifestyle goals that will enable you to reach your performance, performance season, and long-term goals. Also, under *Method*, indicate specifically how you will attain the training and lifestyle goals. Use the Dance Fitness Analysis (see page 25) and your performing attitude profile to assist you in determining what goals to set.

Training goals (in and out of studio)

Technical (double turns, jumps)

1.

Method:

2.

Method:

3.

Method:

Physical (strength, flexibility, stamina)

1.

Method:

2.

Method:

3.

Method:

(continued)

(continued)

Mental (motivation, confidence, intensity, concentration)

1.

Method:

2.

Method:

3.

Method:

Lifestyle goals (sleep, diet, school, work, social)

1.

Method:

2.

Method:

3.

Method:

---

realistic and attainable. If dancers set goals that are too low, high motivation is not necessary because they will reach easy goals with little effort. If your dancers set goals that are too high, they will have little motivation to work toward them because, no matter how hard they try, they will not achieve overly difficult goals. Key questions you need to ask your dancers are, "How committed are you?" and, "Given the amount of time and effort you are willing to expend, what goals are reasonable?"

You and your dancers must also consider whether they have the resources and opportunities to attain their goals. These include access to dance training facilities and adequate instruction, and sufficient time and finances for training and travel. For example, it would probably be unrealistic for a 16-year-old new to dance, who takes ballet classes twice a week, to set a goal of joining the American Ballet Theatre. Martha set her performance season goal of becoming a prima ballerina in her company based upon an examination of her progress over the past five years and lengthy discussions and encouragement from the company's artistic director and dance mistress.

Second, *goals should be specific and concrete.* It is not enough for dancers to say, for example, that they want to have better roles this year. In Martha's case, she identified several key roles she wanted to dance during the season. Dancers should set goals that are clearly stated and measurable, with a particular amount of time in which to achieve them. One of Martha's training goals was to increase her leg strength by 15% by the beginning of the performance season. Assigning a deadline further increased her motivation to achieve this goal.

Third, *dancers should focus on the degree of attainment rather than on the absolute attainment of their goals.* The reality is that not all goals will be reached. Moreover, if your dancers are only concerned with whether or not they reach a goal, they may perceive themselves as failures if they do not reach it. However, though not all goals are reached, chances are dancers will improve as they work toward every goal. By focusing on degree of attainment, even if they do not reach a goal, but improve 50% over their previous level, they are more likely to see themselves as having succeeded. Emphasize that the effort involved in striving for a goal and the improvement toward it is as important as reaching it. One of Martha's performance goals was to dance a leading role in two of the company's productions. She performed a leading role in only one production, but this was one more than she had danced the previous season.

Fourth, *goal setting is a dynamic process that never really ends.* Goals should be reviewed regularly and adjusted as the need arises. It is rarely possible to set perfectly accurate goals. Sometimes your dancers will set goals that are more easily reached than expected. Encourage them to immediately set a new goal toward which to strive. "When you reach a platform, look for the stairs leading up to the next platform" (Holm, 1979, p. 75). Martha worked very hard in her physical training during the off-season and reached her goal of increased leg strength one month prior to the beginning of the performance season. Consequently, she readjusted her goal up to 20% by the season's start. Conversely, your dancers may also set some goals that turn out to be too difficult to achieve in the specified time period. In this case, these goals should be modified to a more realistic level.

Fifth, *once the necessary goals have been set, motivation and commitment can be increased by preparing a written contract.* Goal-setting contracts are explicit statements of dancers' goals and the specific means of attaining them. For contracts to be most effective follow these three guidelines: (a) the contract must be written by the dancer (you may assist your dancer in setting goals, but the goals must be fully accepted by the dancer), (b) the goals must be specific and explicit, and (c) the goals stated in the contract should be made public among your dancer's peers, teachers, and other significant people. Another helpful strategy is to hold periodic individual and group meetings with your dancers to enable them to discuss their goals with you and among themselves.

Finally, goal setting works only if there is regular feedback indicating progress toward a goal. You can provide this feedback in several forms. Have your dancers keep daily dance diaries to record their progress in different areas. Periodically videotape class, rehearsal, and performances to provide clear proof of technical or artistic improvement. Also, give regular goal-related feedback to your dancers to let them know that they are progressing toward their goals. As a general rule for goal feedback, measure and chart any area in which dancers have set goals to furnish them with tangible evidence of advancement.

Regular Training Partners

Dance is an activity that requires many hours of practice to attain a high level of mastery and artistry. Those long hours can sometimes be boring, tiring, and painful. Dancers have difficulty consistently maintaining a high level of motivation by themselves. A useful strategy to help your dancers stay motivated is to pair them with a regular *training partner*. No matter how motivated dancers are, and no matter how hard they train on their own, they will work much harder if someone is pushing them. On any given day, one of your dancers may not be motivated, but if the dancers have partners it is likely that at least one of the pair will be motivated and supportive of the other.

Having a training partner creates a greater feeling of commitment and obligation for dancers to train because someone is depending on them. You can motivate your dancers by having them find a training partner with similar ability and goals, and a compatible training regimen.

Motivational Cues

All dancers have their own ways of motivating themselves. A common means is using *motivational cues*, which are reminders to work hard toward their goals. Motivational cues may come in several forms. They may be meaningful words or phrases, or a list of short-term goals. Motivational cues may also be photographs of favorite or leading dancers. Motivational cues should be placed where your dancers can see them regularly, for example, in their bedrooms and around the studio. Motivational cues provide tangible prompts to your dancers to focus on why they are training so hard and what they need to do to achieve their goals.

Daily Dance Diary

One of the most important sources of satisfaction and motivation for dancers is seeing steady improvements in all aspects of their preparation and performance. Dancers can keep a *dance diary* as a useful means of identifying areas of improvement. A dance diary is composed of daily entries recording a dancer's training, rehearsals, and performances. Entries should consist of an evaluation of each day's class, rehearsal, or performance. Specific topics should include accomplishments and improvement, technical strengths and weaknesses, thoughts and feelings about the day's activities, lifestyle routines such as sleep and diet, progress toward goals, and areas needing future work.

By keeping a regular record of their dance-related activities, dancers learn

(a) their current level of performance,

(b) how close they are to attaining their goals, and

(c) what progress they've made toward the goal.

The dance diary lets them see, in a tangible form, improvement in aspects of their dance. It also assists dancers in setting and adjusting goals.

Motivational Dance Imagery

Dance imagery may be used to increase motivation. Some suggest that having performers imagine themselves performing successfully inspires them to practice more diligently and perform harder. As your dancers warm up, have them imagine themselves working hard, performing well, and reaching their goals. Dance imagery should, most importantly, create feelings of accomplishment and joy. Dance imagery is discussed in greater detail in chapter 5.

Two Daily Questions

Dancers may have difficulty maintaining their training and performance focus and motivation day in and day out. Consequently, remind them of why they are working so hard and what they need to do to reach their goals. To assist in this process, encourage your dancers to ask themselves two questions every day. In the morning, ask, "What can I do today to become the best dancer I can be?" Then, at the end of the day, ask, "Did I do everything possible today to become the best dancer I can be?" These two questions will motivate your dancers to keep foremost in their minds what they need to do to reach their potential and whether they did it.

Center Stage:
Motivating Your Dancers in Class

As instructor, strive to

- offer variety in class,
- make class meaningful to your dancers,
- encourage your dancers to set micro goals for every class,
- ensure that your dancers have mostly successful experiences,
- match the ability of your dancers to the demands of the class, and
- be sensitive to your dancers' motivation during class.

Motivating Dancers in Class

Training to be a dancer is a long, intense, and difficult process. The constant strain of classes, rehearsals and performances can wear a dancer down both physically and mentally. Moreover, the necessary repetitiveness of dance training can become monotonous and tedious.

> Ballet technique is arbitrary and very difficult. It never becomes easy—it becomes possible. The effort involved in making a dancer's body is so long and relentless, in many instances so painful, the effort to maintain the technique so grueling that unless a certain satisfaction is derived from the disciplining and the punishing, the pace could not be maintained. (de Mille, 1952, p. 50)

This description highlights the potential difficulty dancers will have staying motivated. It is important that you seek out ways to motivate and challenge your dancers in the face of such pain and discomfort.

Micro goals.   Dancers often take a class and go through the motions of exercises without purpose. This results in poor quality and lengthier training to make up for the limited gains. Micro goals help instill purpose in training by providing dancers with specific, daily objectives that give focus and direction to each class or rehearsal. Micro goals ensure that both you and your dancers know exactly what they want to accomplish.

Martha, for example, liked to socialize with other dancers in class. This caused her to be poorly focused when executing exercises and rehearsing a role. She also had to repeat skills to perform them adequately. With a written goal of what she would be focusing on for each exercise, she paid greater attention to her exercises and increased the quality of her class time and rehearsal.

Ask your dancers when they arrive at the studio if they have micro goals. If they do not offer a specific objective for that day's class, they should establish one before they participate. With a clearly stated micro goal, dancers will have purpose and direction for every class and rehearsal, resulting in an increase in the quality and a decrease in the quantity of training.

Variety in class.   There are few things worse for motivation than routine, monotonous classes. They should be fun and interesting, stressing variety. Dancers can learn a new technique several ways. Be creative in devising motivating ways for your dancers to learn. Also, make opportunities available for personal achievement and developing self-confidence.

Make class meaningful.   If dancers see no point in performing a particular exercise, they will not be motivated to work hard at it. Moreover, the rationale for an exercise may not always be apparent. To ensure full understanding and commitment, explain the purpose of the exercise. In particular, show how the exercise relates to your dancers' goals. For example, demonstrate how the exercise will enable them to learn a sequence of movements for certain roles in an upcoming production. A valuable method to increase commitment is to ask your dancers for suggestions on the lesson focus and exercises. This technique enhances involvement and makes dancers feel more personally responsible for their efforts.

Ensure successful experiences.   Dancers are typically motivated to engage in activities in which they often succeed because the experience reinforces and enhances their self-confidence and sense of competence. Conversely, dancers have little motivation to participate in activities in which they usually fail. As a result, it is important that you ensure that dancers succeed most of the time in class. The likelihood of success among your dancers depends on two things. One, you must have a clear understanding of the abilities of your dancers. If you do not know their skill levels, you may be asking them to engage futilely in exercises of which they are not capable. Two, you must carefully plan class lessons consistent with their skill levels. Additionally, be flexible in your lesson plan, so if an exercise is too difficult, a new one may be substituted that is more likely to produce success.

Ability must equal demands.   Csikzentmihalyi (1975) suggests that there are three possible outcomes when an individual participates in an activity. First, if the demands of the task are greater than one's ability, the experience will cause anxiety, and motivation will decrease. Second, if one's ability is greater than the demands of the activity, boredom will result, and motivation will again decline. Third, if the demands of the task match one's ability, the individual will be challenged, and motivation will remain high. To make this match, you must have a clear understanding of your dancers' abilities and the demands of the exercises you give them.

Be sensitive to class motivation.　During all classes and rehearsals, you should be sensitive to the motivation levels of your dancers and respond accordingly. Dancers will often indirectly convey that they are not motivated. Sloppy execution, irrelevant conversation, lack of attention to your instruction, and low energy are all strong indicators that the class plan or a particular exercise may not be motivating your dancers. Always be an active *and* re-active participant during class and rehearsals, and be willing to adjust your program based on the feedback.

By providing a motivating environment, you create an atmosphere that enables your dancers to fulfill their potential. More importantly, you promote healthy attitudes, enjoyment, satisfaction, and interest. Your dancers will develop an enduring love and appreciation for dance that will motivate them to participate for many years to come. You'll know you have accomplished this when your dancers echo the feeling of Fredova when she stated, "I have practiced for three hours. I am exhausted, and I feel wonderful" (de Mille, 1952, p. 50).

ENCORE

Motivation involves the ability to initiate and persist at a task. Applied to dance, motivation is the capacity for dancers to persist in the face of boredom, fatigue, and pain.

High motivation produces total preparation, which leads to optimal performance. Motivation influences physical conditioning, technical training, mental preparation, and lifestyle.

Dancers are motivated by different things, such as high aspirations, social interaction, and satisfaction from mastering skills. You must identify the motivational needs of each of your dancers and motivate them accordingly. Motivation influences participation and performance.

Evidence of motivation in your dancers includes having high energy and enthusiasm for class and rehearsal, putting 100% effort into their dance, completing all aspects of the training regimen, and having clearly defined goals. Signs of low motivation include having little eagerness in class or rehearsal, rarely expending full effort, taking unneeded days off, cutting short training routines, and having unclear goals.

The Dance Fitness Analysis helps dancers identify their strengths and weaknesses in order to set more relevant goals for themselves.

Goal setting is an effective means of increasing motivation because it guides dancers' actions, directs the output of effort, and encourages learning new ways to improve. Dancers should set five types of goals: long-term, performance season, performance, training, and lifestyle.

Goals should be challenging, realistic, specific, and concrete. Dancers should focus on achieving a degree of, rather than absolute attainment of goals. Give dancers regular feedback indicating progress toward their goals.

Other strategies for dancers to use to increase motivation include having a training partner, posting motivational cues such as words, phrases, and photos, keeping a daily dance diary, using motivational imagery, and asking the two daily motivational questions.

Techniques to increase motivation in class include having dancers set micro goals, using variety in class exercises, making each class meaningful, ensuring successful experiences, matching dancers' abilities to the demands of the class, and being sensitive to the motivational levels of your dancers during class.

2

Self-Confidence

The dancer with conviction has power; many a dance of poor quality has been "put across" just by the superb belief of the performer in the work. . . . If you believe in yourself, everybody else probably will, too. (Humphrey, 1951, p. 84)

Dress Rehearsal:
Building Self-Confidence

Denise is a 21-year-old dance major and jazz dancer at a large state university. She has a leading role in the dance department's spring production. Due to a heavy course load and a lengthy bout with the flu, Denise is behind in her rehearsals and is having serious doubts about her ability to perform, despite your belief that she is more than capable. During rehearsals, she has been depressed, frustrated, and very negative about her dancing, which has slowed her learning the role.

1. What has caused Denise's decline in self-confidence? What other psychological factors are being affected by it?
2. How would you address her current difficulties?

Self-confidence, the second level of the performing attitude pyramid, may be the most important psychological factor that influences dance performance and is an integral part of the PPEP. Self-confidence in dance can be defined as how strongly dancers believe they can learn and execute a skill or perform a certain role. Dancers' self-confidence is critical because even if they are physically and technically capable of performing, but do not believe they can perform well, they will not use their abilities. Consequently, you must not only teach technical and artistic skills, but also instill in your dancers the belief in their ability to perform those skills.

PROBLEMS OF LOW SELF-CONFIDENCE

Self-confidence influences performance directly and indirectly. For example, Susan, a 17-year-old ballet dancer, is gifted but has little confidence in her ability. This lack of self-confidence hurts her in a number of ways, mentally and emotionally. Her low self-confidence caused her to engage in negative and defeating self-talk. Susan often said things like, "I just can't learn this new movement" and "I know I am going to blow it in tomorrow night's performance."

This negativity caused Susan to fall into a vicious cycle of low self-confidence and poor performance. The cycle started with doubts about her ability.

In turn she did not dance as well as she was capable of dancing. Her inadequate performance confirmed her initial doubts and further decreased her self-confidence. Subsequently she performed even worse. Eventually, her negative thinking and poor performances fed on each other until Susan believed she was incapable of performing at all (see Figure 2.1).

Self-confidence is significantly related to anxiety. Dancers with high self-confidence tend to be relaxed during a performance and dance well, while those with low self-confidence become anxious which impairs their performance. Susan was very nervous before and during dance performances so it was even more likely that Susan would dance poorly. The next chapter discusses how excessive anxiety inhibits performance in a variety of ways.

Furthermore, low self-confidence produces negative emotions, such as depression, anger, guilt, and frustration, all of which hurt dance performance. In fact, Susan would often become so depressed and frustrated during rehearsal that she would simply give up trying to learn a new role.

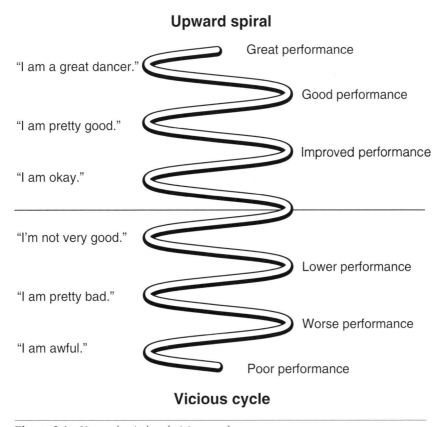

Figure 2.1   Upward spiral and vicious cycle.

Dancers with low self-confidence tend to focus on negative or irrelevant things rather than on what will enable them to perform their best. In Susan's case, while auditioning for a role she would often think about competing dancers, her fear of dancing poorly, and of her parents' disappointment if she didn't get the part. Instead, she should have been concentrating on the technique and artistry associated with the role.

To summarize, Susan is a talented dancer with low self-confidence, caught in a vicious cycle of negative thinking and performance, anxious, depressed, frustrated, and unable to adequately concentrate. The unfortunate effect of this chain is that Susan lost her motivation to dance; didn't enjoy class, rehearsal, and performances; and, quite simply, didn't enjoy dancing anymore. Since she no longer finds dance rewarding, she will probably quit dancing altogether.

BENEFITS OF HIGH SELF-CONFIDENCE

In contrast to Susan, David is a 16-year-old dancer who, though not as talented as Susan, has considerable confidence in his dancing ability. This self-confidence produces a chain opposite to that experienced by Susan.

David's self-confidence produced positive thinking and self-talk, such as, "I am going to work really hard to get this role" and "I'm going to dance my best tonight." This positive attitude generated an upward spiral of high self-confidence and good performance, in turn producing more confidence and better performances.

Since David is so confident, he is relaxed about his performances, and as a result, is able to dance well. He experienced positive emotions during rehearsal and performances, including happiness, joy, and excitement. Also because David had few concerns about his performing he was able to concentrate on those things that enable him to perform his best, including technique, artistry, and stage cues. This chain of self-confidence resulted in David's motivation to rehearse and perform, and tremendous satisfaction from his dance.

DEVELOPING SELF-CONFIDENCE

The foundation for developing self-confidence in your dancers involves two steps. First, you must help them become aware of their dance-related thinking. Second, you must assist them in developing a positive and constructive way of thinking about their dancing.

Many dancers think that self-confidence is something they either have or do not have. To the contrary, self-confidence can be learned, especially with younger dancers. Dancers are often their own worst enemy. This is a serious problem because when they go on stage they are alone, and if they aren't on their own side, they are certain to falter. The goal then of developing self-confidence is for dancers to become their own best ally.

Now that you have identified each dancer's self-confidence using performing attitude profiling, the next step is to show them how to develop their self-confidence to a level that will enhance performance. The following techniques are simple and practical, and can easily be incorporated into regular dance class and rehearsal. As with technical skills, building self-confidence takes practice, so it is critical that you make these skills, and others described in this book, a regular part of your interaction with your dancers.

Performance Success

The most direct and effective means of building self-confidence in your dancers is through successful performance. In designing lesson plans, teaching new skills, and assigning roles, ensure that each dancer is likely to achieve success. A general rule is that dancers should perform successfully at least 75% of the time.

Another direct way to develop self-confidence in your dancers is to enable them to clearly measure and recognize improvement in their dancing. Have dancers establish specific performance improvement goals. Then place greater emphasis on improvement than on performance outcome.

Walk the Walk

Outstanding dancers carry themselves, move, and walk differently than less gifted dancers. This is due partially to their higher level of self-confidence. Dancers can influence how they think and feel by how they carry themselves. It is difficult to think and feel down when their body is up, and hard to think and feel up when their body is down.

Thus the first technique for developing self-confidence in your dancers is to have them *walk the walk*. Before, during, and after class have them exaggerate two extremes of walking. First have them move around the studio with their head and eyes down, shoulders hunched, and feet dragging. Ask them how they feel. Then have them walk with their head high, chin up, eyes forward, and shoulders back, and ask how they feel. Next, tell them to say things that are contradictory to how they are carrying themselves. For example, if they are walking the "up" walk, have them say things like, "I can't do this" and "I am a terrible dancer." They will find that it is difficult; when the body is up, their thoughts and feelings will also be positive.

Talk the Talk

How dancers talk to themselves directly affects their self-confidence. Begin shaping the way they think and what they say to themselves and others about their dance performances by encouraging positive self-talk. Similar to having them walk the walk, have them *talk the talk*. You can teach your dancers four types of positive self-talk. First, *self-encouragement* consists of general statements that are realistic, positive, and supportive, such as, "I'm performing really well" and "I'm getting better every day." Second, *effort control* involves motivational statements, such as, "I'm working hard" and "Keep focused on the task at hand." Third, *performance goal achievement* consists of statements related to specific objectives, such as, "That turn was excellent, now I must work on the leap" and "I only made one mistake that time, now I will get it right." Finally, general positive self-talk consists of global positive statements like, "I did that better than I expected" and "great rehearsal."

A simple and unobtrusive exercise you can use to start this process is to ask your dancers how they will dance in an upcoming class, rehearsal, or performance. Even at the highest levels of dance, performers will give answers like, "I may dance okay," "I don't know, we'll see," and "I hope I don't blow it." These answers are negative and self-defeating, feeding into the vicious cycle. If your dancers do not give a positive response, encourage them to say something positive, even if they don't believe it. If they consistently practice positive thinking and self-talk with conviction, they eventually will believe it *and* do it. This is the first step in teaching your dancers to control their thinking and self-talk. Be gentle but firm, and begin the process of getting them to talk more positively.

Thought-Stopping

A psychological technique often used to train positive thinking and develop self-confidence is *thought-stopping*. This strategy is effective in helping dancers become aware of their negative thinking and showing them how to replace it with positive thinking. It is composed of several steps.

First, dancers should list the negative statements they think or make during classes, rehearsals, and performances. You, and the class, can help each dancer recall commonly spoken negative statements. Second, dancers should list positive statements that could replace the negative ones. For example, a dancer might often say, "I danced horribly at rehearsal today." Next time she says this, she should say, "stop" or "positive," and replace it with, "I know what I did wrong today and will work hard to dance better tomorrow." The latter statement is both positive and motivating. Positive replacement statements should be realistic. For instance, if dancers had a poor rehearsal, it would not be reasonable for them to say, "I had a great rehearsal and I am dancing very well." Rather, they should say something positive that can motivate them in the future (see the Thought-Stopping Exercise worksheet).

Dancer's Litany

A common mistake dancers make in dealing with mental skills, such as self-confidence, is that they wait for something bad to happen before they start working on their mental preparation. This makes little sense. After all, dancers don't wait to get hurt before they do physical conditioning, or put off technical work until they develop a technical problem. Rather, in both cases, they work hard all along to prevent problems. This preventive approach should also be used in developing self-confidence.

Thought-Stopping Exercise

Directions: In the space below, list some common negative thoughts you have, where and when they typically occur, and positive statements to replace them.

Negative thoughts	Time, place, situation	Positive replacements
1.		
2.		
3.		
4.		
5.		
6.		
7.		
8.		
9.		
10.		

One effective preventive technique is known as the *dancer's litany.* A litany is a group of positive statements dancers can say to themselves or out loud that teach positive self-talk and increase self-confidence. Dancers can practice building their self-confidence *before* they lose it. Figure 2.2 contains an example of a typical dancer's litany. Teach your dancers to use the litany by including it as part of your class time. For example, the litany can be recited prior to and following class. When used at the beginning of class, it increases positive attitudes and motivation, enhancing the quality of class time. When used leaving class, it also gives the dancers a final positive boost. Also encourage them to say the litany on their own, preferably when waking up and again before bedtime.

It is not enough to just say the litany. They must say it with conviction. Dancers who don't really believe the statements they are making don't sound very convincing. To get dancers to convince themselves of these statements, have them say them like they believe them. When dancers use the litany, and have positive experiences to reinforce the litany statements, they gradually *do* come to believe them, and increase their self-confidence. Dancers should personalize their litanies to include statements that have particular meaning for them, enhancing the litany's value to each dancer.

I love to dance.

I am a great dancer.

I always think and talk positively.

I expect to feel pressure and that's okay, because I know how to handle it.

I am confident, relaxed, and focused when I dance.

I always work my hardest in class and rehearsal.

I will be the best dancer I can be.

Note. Develop your own dancer's litany, emphasizing statements that are important to you.

Figure 2.2   Dancer's litany.

Positive Key Words

Dancers often have difficulty trying to develop their self-confidence because during a rehearsal or performance they become so focused on the pressures of performing that they simply forget to work on their positive thinking. A helpful technique is to create one or two words or phrases, called *positive key words*. By saying them, dancers will focus their attention on positive thinking and self-talk rather than on negative aspects of the rehearsal or performance. Examples of key words include "positive," "up," and "believe." Key words are very personal, so you should help your dancers create key words that are personally meaningful to each of them. Have your dancers write their key words and post them in their rooms, on their lockers, around the studio, or on a piece of clothing. The idea is to constantly remind dancers to focus on positive aspects of their performance. As discussed in later chapters, key words can be used to focus attention on motivational, physical, and technical aspects of performance.

Teach Dancers to Think Rationally and Objectively

During class or rehearsal, dancers can often become angry and frustrated when they have trouble learning a key skill or element. They react this way because they are thinking critically and emotionally, a reaction that is self-defeating and counter-productive.

Help them overcome this response by teaching them to think rationally and objectively, that is, to think like you in a teaching role. When a student is struggling, how do you respond? You identify the problem area, indicate the correction, and then have the student focus on the correction until it is mastered. Your students are capable of doing the same thing given proper guidance and encouragement. Have them engage in that same objective evaluation process. With practice, students will adopt this procedure and benefit from the results. Instead of dwelling on past mistakes and becoming discouraged, they will be more positive and motivated, knowing how to overcome the mistake in the future.

Teach Dancers to Trust Their Ability

As discussed earlier, in addition to teaching technique, an important part of dance instruction is instilling in your dancers belief in their dancing ability. What comes from this belief is an underlying trust in their ability to perform on any given day. Trust is defined as "Letting go of conscious controlling tendencies and allowing automatic processes . . . to execute the motor skill" (Moore & Stevenson, 1991, p. 282). In other words, it is the belief in their capacity to execute in performance what has been learned in practice. As

Deborah Hay urged her dancers, "Trust yourself. Use the images to take you as far out and as far in as you will go. Trust yourself . . . to feel everything there is" (Banes, 1980, p. 125).

There is a time and a place for every aspect of the dance experience. For example, class and rehearsal are the appropriate settings for you and your dancers to analyze and critique their dance. However, when it is performance time, it is no longer suitable to question, doubt, analyze, or think about technique. Unfortunately, dancers have a tendency to do just that. This excessive cognitive activity, called jamming, results in a decline in self-confidence, an increase in anxiety, and poor execution of the required skills. Rather, at this stage, dancers must set aside these concerns and trust their ability to perform the best they can, letting the learned sequence of skills emerge automatically and without conscious control.

Dancers who focus solely on technique may execute skills well, but their overall performance and artistry suffers. If dancers haven't fully perfected a technique or sequence of movements by the time of the performance, they will not successfully execute them. Teach them that whatever ability they bring to the performance, they should believe in it, and do the best they can with what they have.

Teaching dancers to trust begins by showing them the appropriate time and place for focusing on technique (class and rehearsal), and for trusting their ability (performance). As dancers become more self-confident, they will question themselves less, and like the upward spiral, trust in their ability will become self-perpetuating.

ADDITIONAL STRATEGIES TO BUILD SELF-CONFIDENCE

Dancers will often look to you to determine how they should think, feel, and behave. They look to you as a role model. Consequently, it is important that you convey confidence in all of your contact with them. If you show confidence in their ability and effort, they are more likely to internalize that belief.

Verbal Persuasion and Reward

Verbal persuasion is another effective technique in enhancing self-confidence. Often, when learning new skills, dancers have little confidence in their ability to execute them because they have had no direct experience performing them. To motivate dancers, you must convince them that they can perform the skills successfully. Trust is a critical factor here. If they do not have faith in your knowledge of their ability to succeed, they will not feel comfortable trying the new skills. You must be truly confident that they can succeed, because if they fail in their efforts, they will lose confidence in themselves and in you.

 ## Center Stage:
Developing Self-Confidence

Have your dancers do the following:

- Walk the walk: Walk and move like a star.
- Talk the talk: Think and talk like a star.
- Practice thought-stopping: If they start to think negatively, say "stop," then replace it with something positive.
- Say the dancer's litany every morning and night, and before class, rehearsal, and performance.
- Think positive key words and look at positive messages.
- Think objectively and rationally: Analyze past mistakes, focus on future corrections.
- Trust their abilities: Let their bodies do what they know how to do.

As instructor, strive to do the following:

- Use verbal persuasion and reward: Convince your dancers they can succeed, then reward success.
- Reframe failure: Teach them to interpret failure in a positive way.
- Use other dancers as role models: Point out similar dancers who are successful.

Furthermore, following successful performances you should liberally *reward* your dancers. This regular reinforcement will motivate them to continue to work hard and will, in time, be internalized, thus increasing their self-confidence.

Reframing Failure

Dancers have a tendency to internalize failure, that is, they believe that failure is due to a lack of innate ability. This is not a healthy perspective because ability is not readily controllable or changeable. As a result, when dancers do fail, you must help them *reframe* the experience as being due to lack of effort or insufficient time. By doing so, they will maintain their motivation to work on the problem area, increasing the likelihood that, in time, they will succeed.

Reframing will also benefit your dancers' experience of intensity. As discussed in chapter 3, the presence or absence of intensity ("I'm too nervous to dance well" or "I don't have the energy to dance well") is often interpreted negatively by dancers. They take this to mean that they lack confidence and motivation to perform well. Reframe these physical sensations in a positive manner. If dancers say they are nervous, explain that these feelings indicate that their bodies are getting prepared for performance, and these physical signs mean they are ready to perform their best. If dancers lack intensity, tell them this indicates that they are confident in their ability. These reinterpretations increase self-confidence because the dancers perceive themselves as prepared to dance well.

Other Dancers as Role Models

Using the example of other dancers may also improve your dancers' confidence. This approach, termed *vicarious experience*, shows dancers that other dancers who are similar to them have been successful, developing the belief that, "if they can do it, so can I."

ENCORE

Self-confidence may be the most important psychological factor that influences dancers' performances.

It is essential that you not only teach the necessary skills, but also instill in your dancers the belief in their ability to perform those skills.

Help your dancers become aware of how they think and teach them how they can positively alter their thoughts.

Ensure performance success in class, rehearsal, and performance. Dancers should succeed at least 75% of the time.

Assist your dancers in developing their self-confidence by having them walk the walk, talk the talk, practice thought-stopping, and repeat the dancer's litany and key words.

Be a positive role model and use other dancers as role models. Apply verbal persuasion, use liberal rewards, and reframe failure.

Developing self-confidence takes time and effort.

3

Intensity

The appearance of intensity may come from their devotion to what they are doing. It can give the look of being highly involved in the moment, that urgency that doing something precisely in the largest possible way can provoke. (Merce Cunningham in Cohen, 1974, p. 199)

Dress Rehearsal:
Controlling Intensity

Rudy is a 24-year-old ballet dancer who recently joined a major metropolitan company. Due to a spate of injuries to several of the leading male dancers, Rudy is required to assume a demanding role in the company's upcoming production. Having just arrived, he does not know any of the dancers and is a bit in awe of the artistic director, the size of the company, and its facilities. During rehearsals, Rudy has been very nervous and has been struggling with the role.

1. What has caused Rudy's nervousness? What kind of symptoms would you expect to see during rehearsal?
2. How would you address Rudy's difficulties?

As the performing attitude pyramid illustrates, when the time of the performance arrives, another factor, intensity, takes center stage and plays a key role in the PPEP. *Intensity* refers to the dancer's degree of physiological preparedness prior to performing. Intensity is characterized by changes in an individual's physiological state, such as heart rate, blood flow, and adrenaline production, and may range from very low, as in a deep sleep, to very high, as in extreme fear. Dancers may experience intensity positively, as increased strength, stamina, agility, and heightened sensory acuity. As Twyla Tharp (1992) expressed,

> I began to discriminate between fear and excitement. The two, though very close, are completely different. Fear is negative excitement, choking your imagination. Real excitement produces an energy that overcomes apprehension and makes you want to close in on your goal. (p. 79)

Unfortunately, intensity also may be perceived negatively, as muscle tension, breathing difficulty, and loss of coordination. Paul Taylor, when asked if he got nervous before a performance responded, "Yes, I always did. Extreme jitters. I never got over that" (Lyle, 1977, p. 119).

WHAT IS INTENSITY?

Other terms that have been used synonymously with intensity are arousal, anxiety, and nervousness. Whereas arousal has sexual connotations and anxiety and nervousness have negative ones, intensity can be experienced pos-itively or negatively—either inhibiting or facilitating dance performance.

Intensity is the most critical factor prior to performance because no matter how confident or motivated, or technically or physically prepared your danc-ers are, if their bodies are not at an optimal level of intensity, they will simply not be able to perform their best. Moreover, too little or too much intensity will adversely affect performance. In addition, intensity may also influence dancers' artistry.

Optimal intensity is an individual response; not one ideal level of intensity exists for all dancers. For example, some dancers may perform at their best when they are at a very low level of intensity (totally relaxed). Others may dance their best at a very high level of intensity (extremely energized).

In 1908, Yerkes and Dodson proposed the inverted-U theory of arousal, which suggests that increases in arousal will produce commensurate im-provement in performance, but only to a point, after which greater arousal will inhibit performance (see Figure 3.1). "I'm a very nervous performer, but I need that nervous edge. You can easily become far too casual, of course, but I think there must be a happy medium" (Jennifer Penney in Doob, 1982, p. 12).

Oxendine (1970) further suggested that different physical activities require different levels of arousal based on their task complexity. Specifically, he indicated that highly complex activities requiring fine motor control with a

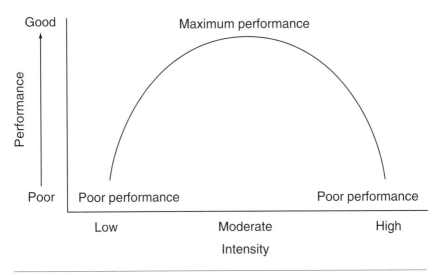

Figure 3.1   Yerkes-Dodson's inverted-U theory of intensity.
From "Arousal-Performance Relationships" by D.M. Landers and S.H. Boutcher. In *Applied Sport Psychology: Personal Growth to Peak Performance* (pp. 163–184) by J. Williams (Ed.), 1986, Palo Alto, CA: Mayfield.

minimal amount of strength would need very low levels of arousal because greater arousal would interfere with the necessary fine motor coordination. In contrast, activities involving only gross motor skills and great amounts of strength would require high levels of arousal that produce increased adrenaline and associated gains in strength.

Because dance involves relatively fine motor skills as well as strength and stamina, dancers require a moderate level of intensity to perform their best. As such, intensity is needed to provide strength and stamina, but not so much intensity that it interferes with the fine movements common in many forms of dance. As Steve Paxton expressed, "The adrenaline should come . . . and then it should have a calm on top of it, so that the kick of adrenaline . . . can be enjoyed, and calmly watched" (Banes, 1980, p. 66). Make it your goal to assist your dancers in identifying and attaining their optimal level of intensity. But first you need to gain a greater understanding of what causes different levels of intensity and how to recognize these levels in your dancers.

SYMPTOMS AND CAUSES OF INTENSITY

Intensity manifests itself in a number of physical and psychological symptoms, some apparent and some subtle. These symptoms may positively or negatively influence dance performance, depending on the individual dancer's response.

In addition to dancers' own internal responses, intensity is also affected by a variety of interpersonal and situational factors. Fear of failure and evaluation will directly influence intensity levels. Environmental and social variables prior to and during the performance, such as the importance of the role, the performance site, and who is in the audience will influence intensity as will physical elements including general health, level of fatigue, and injuries.

Symptoms of Over-Intensity

"You can't be too nervous because it robs you of everything, it robs the muscles. You stand and feel weak", states Tanaquil LeClercq (Newman, 1982, p. 158). Prior to and during a performance, learn to identify symptoms of *over-intensity* in your dancers. You can then take steps to assist them in reducing their intensity to an optimal level.

Over-intensity manifests itself in several ways. The most apparent symptoms are physical reactions that include extreme muscle tension, shaking muscles, difficulty breathing, and excessive perspiration. "Tension, never seen previously at rehearsals, suddenly becomes evident in the neck and limbs of the dancers" (Sande, 1977, p. 6). Other symptoms are psychological and emotional in nature and may reveal themselves as negative self-talk ("I know I will screw up the lift"), irrational thinking ("If I dance badly, my family and friends will disown me"), and emotional feelings of fear and dread. Other symptoms may not be apparent until the performance: fatigue, decreased coordination, and difficulty breathing. In addition, "Balance, apparently secure in the studio, is destroyed because of nervousness" (Sande, 1977, p. 6).

Educate your dancers to recognize less overt indications of over-intensity. Symptoms you may not be aware of, but your dancers will, include stomach butterflies, mistakes during warm-up, and an extreme narrowing of concentration away from an effective performance focus to negative thoughts and feelings caused by over-intensity.

Causes of Over-Intensity

> The older I got, the more frightened I got, because the more responsibility was on my shoulders. When you're a nobody, you dance. When you get discovered, and they start, for instance, applauding when you come out on-stage, before you've done anything. That's always death. (LeClercq in Newman, 1982, p. 158)

Landers and Boutcher (1986) specify five areas of appraisal that can lead to an intensity reaction:

- Demands of the situation
- Individual's resources to effectively manage the demands
- Consequences of the situation
- Meaning that is placed on the consequences
- Recognition of bodily reactions

The audition is a common setting in which this appraisal process may cause over-intensity. As choreographer Kenneth Green stated, "Auditions in general are uncomfortable experiences. But for children, they can be frightening" (Greenhill, 1992, p. 56). For example, Richard, a 17-year-old dancer who was auditioning for a position in a prestigious company, perceived that the requirements of his assigned role (demands) were greater than his ability (resources) to fulfill the role. He believed that he would fail in his performance (consequences) and it would ruin his dance career (meaning). Finally, as he thought about these things, he became increasingly agitated and uncomfortable (recognition of bodily reactions), further elevating his intensity to a debilitating level.

Other factors may exacerbate this reaction, such as unfamiliarity with the situation, the occurrence of unexpected events, and worry over uncontrollable aspects of the situation. For instance, because Richard was new to the company, he was unfamiliar with the other dancers, the dance mistress, the rehearsal studio, and the performance hall. In addition, less than an hour before the performance, he could not find a part of his costume. Finally, instead of focusing on what he needed to do to dance his best, he was thinking about the other dancers, the critics in the audience, and what the artistic director would think of him. These thoughts and events added to his feelings of uncertainty, increasing his level of intensity.

Symptoms of Under-Intensity

Learn to identify signs of *under-intensity* in your dancers prior to performances as well. Because decreased intensity is less apparent, you must teach your dancers to be aware of the more subtle signals. On a subtle level, dancers should be aware of low heart rate, lack of adrenaline, absence of energy and alertness, and difficulty focusing attention on their roles. On a manifest level, look for dancers who appear lethargic, seem to lack interest in what is going on around them, and aren't concentrating on the performance.

Causes of Under-Intensity

Due to the inherent pressures associated with performing, under-intensity is not a common occurrence. However, it may be evident in some of your dancers and in some performances. Contributing factors to under-intensity include overconfidence, lack of interest and motivation, physical fatigue, and high ability coupled with low role demands. Helin (1987), in his study of the Finnish National Ballet, reports that under-intensity is evident among professional ballet dancers during shows that are performed many times.

For example, Marilyn, a 28-year-old, 10-year veteran of a company, found that though she could reach optimal intensity for important roles at major performances, she often lacked intensity when she had a small supporting role in a minor production. Because of her dance experience, Marilyn was very confident in her ability to perform the small roles but was not very motivated to prepare for and perform them, wishing she could sit them out. Because she is a gifted dancer, she was not challenged by the demands of the minor roles. This lack of intensity resulted in unnecessary mistakes and a lack of artistry and technical precision in her performances.

IDENTIFYING OPTIMAL INTENSITY

A variety of inventories have been developed to measure different forms of intensity. However, they focus on the negative effects of excessive intensity and give little consideration to the manifestations of inadequate intensity or identifying optimal intensity. The intensity factor in the performing attitude personal profile will provide you and your dancers with a general measure of their ability to reach and maintain optimal intensity.

You also need to identify the differences between your dancers' optimal and non-optimal levels of intensity. You can accomplish this process in two steps. First, using the Intensity Identification worksheet, have your dancers recall the times when they performed their best. Ask them the following questions:

- How did they feel physically? For example, were they energized and were their hearts pounding?
- What were their thoughts and feelings just prior to the performances?

The purpose of this exercise is to recognize the factors that were present when they danced well. The psychological and physiological factors present at each successful performance will typically be consistent.

Next, have your dancers remember when they performed poorly. Ask them the same questions. This exercise enables your dancers to discriminate between important factors that were present when they danced well vs. poorly. They can then take steps to reproduce those factors associated with good performances.

CONTROLLING OVER-INTENSITY

Now that you have shown your dancers how to identify their optimal and non-optimal levels of intensity, teach them to control their intensity so it will be at its optimal level when performance time arrives.

When over-intensity occurs prior to a performance it can be addressed at several levels and be worked on at various times, such as during rehearsal and just before taking the stage.

Changing Thought and Behavior to Reduce Over-Intensity

As the five areas of appraisal presented by Landers and Boutcher (1986) indicate, over-intensity is most often caused by negative, inaccurate, or extreme thinking about a situation. Consequently, a good place to begin controlling over-intensity is at its source, that is, by altering the thinking process. Dancers' perceptions that they do not have the ability to cope effectively, indicate a basic lack of self-confidence. By developing their self-confidence, dancers may inhibit over-intensity by evaluating each situation positively and accurately. Use the self-confidence building techniques described in chapter 2 to accomplish this.

Intensity Identification

Directions: In the space below, indicate what situations and personal factors are related to your best and worst performances. Then, at the bottom, summarize the positive and negative performance factors that distinguish your best and worst performances.

Factor	Best Performances	Worst Performances
Performance site		
Production		
Performance level		
Thoughts		
Emotions		
Physical state		

Positive performance factors:

Negative performance factors:

Rationally assess performance. Assist your dancers to rationally assess their upcoming performance by discussing the five appraisal areas with them individually and as a group. Often, young dancers become so overwhelmed by the approaching performance that they lose perspective and cannot perceive the situation objectively. As mentioned, this may lead to extreme or irrational thinking, which further increases intensity. For example, one young dancer preparing for an audition said, "I know I'm not as good as some of the other girls. They do the steps just right and look perfect doing them. I'm so nervous about doing something wrong, I know I'm going to mess up" (Greenhill, 1992, p. 57). Ease this debilitating process by providing your dancers with the perspective they are unable to perceive. Typically, show them another way of viewing the situation, where they can recognize the extremity of their thinking and accept the more realistic perspective, thus decreasing intensity levels.

As mentioned in the section on the causes of over-intensity, three factors may exacerbate the negative thinking process: Unfamiliarity with the situation, the occurrence of unexpected events, and focusing on uncontrollable events. You and your dancers can significantly reduce potential negative effects by addressing them well before the performance.

Unfamiliar situations. The best way to prevent or alleviate the effects of an unfamiliar situation is to make it familiar. Unfamiliarity may occur in several ways. Not knowing the physical environment may cause stress in your dancers. "Slippery stages were the terror of my life" (Astaire, 1984, p. 71). The best solution for this problem is to give your dancers an opportunity to familiarize themselves with the performance setting, ideally through rehearsal on the performance stage.

The addition of an audience on opening night can also cause stress. "There is no question that the presence of an audience affects performers. The excitement generated raises the adrenaline level of the body, and a heightened awareness . . . can be the thing that destroys performance" (Sande, 1977, p. 6). To familiarize their dancers with performing before a crowd, the Finnish National Ballet would conduct their final rehearsals in front of an audience (Helin, 1987). Although this direct experience is not always possible, simply allowing the dancers to attend another performance at the facility or walk around it may be helpful. The dancers can then combine their experience of the facility with dance imagery (see chapter 5) to see themselves performing there. In addition, you, or dancers who have been there previously, can describe some of the critical physical aspects of the setting.

Dancers can use these same strategies to familiarize themselves with other aspects of the performance setting. For example, if the upcoming performance is the first for several new members of the company, familiarize them with the typical activity backstage, audience responses, media coverage, and stage entrances, exits, and crossovers. Developing a mentoring system with more experienced dancers will benefit the new dancers and free you to attend to other responsibilities.

Unexpected events.   The occurrence of unexpected events prior to and during performances can also cause over-intensity. The most effective means of handling this problem is to prevent or minimize unexpected incidents. This does not mean that you can prevent all problems from arising during a performance. But you can prevent them from being totally unexpected, and from causing stress. Meet with your dancers, have them identify all of the things that can go wrong at a performance, then have them propose solutions (see Table 3.1). Even though difficulties will still arise, instead of panicking, the dancers will not be surprised by the problem and have a plan for solving it, keeping stress low and intensity at a healthy level.

Table 3.1   Expect the Unexpected

Unexpected event	Plan
Late arrival to performance site	*Have shortened preperformance routine.*
Forget clothing or accessory	*Pack extra gear.*
Worn dance slippers	*Have backup slippers properly broken in.*
No rehearsal space	*Have alternative physical warm up routine.*
Poor floor surface	*Stay relaxed and focused; stay warmed-up.*
Change in schedule	*Repeat preperformance routine.*
Role change	*Stay calm; run through role change.*

Uncontrollable events.   Dancers spend considerable time worrying about things over which they have little control. This is a fruitless endeavor because not only can they not influence those things, but worrying about them creates significant stress. Much of what occurs in the dance world is outside of a dancer's control. Moreover, there is only one thing truly within their control: themselves. As such, they should only focus on themselves, specifically, what they need to do to perform their best (see Table 3.2).

When you see dancers worrying about things, ask them several questions. First, is this something that is within their control? If it is, ask them what they can do to relieve the problem, and help them develop a plan to do so. If it is not, ask them what in the situation they can control, have them focus on that, and help them find a way to alleviate the problem.

Table 3.2   What Can You Control?

Controllable	Uncontrollable
Your behavior	Others' attitudes, thoughts, emotions, motivation, behavior
Physical condition	Other dancers' performances
Motivation/effort	Choreographer
Attitude	Music
Thoughts	Lighting
Emotions	Performance space
Costume	Stage set
Preparation	Last minute changes
Performance	

Important: Do *not* worry about those things over which you have no control! Focus on those things that you can control.

Center Stage: Changing Thought and Behavior to Reduce Over-Intensity

Have your dancers

- practice positive self-talk: no negative thoughts,
- rationally assess performance,
- become familiar with new situations,
- expect the unexpected, and
- focus on what they can control.

Changing Physiology to Reduce Over-Intensity

Despite the best efforts to prevent over-intensity by changing thinking and behavior, due to the inherent pressure of a performance, some dancers will still experience over-intensity. Consequently, you should also provide them with simple and practical techniques to control their physical state that they may use prior to performance to attain their optimal level of intensity.

Breathing.   Perhaps the simplest, yet most important, technique to reduce intensity is controlled breathing. When dancers are under stress and experiencing high levels of intensity, the breathing system contracts, providing an inadequate supply of oxygen. Dancers backstage often take short, choppy breaths. Breathing affects dancers physically because their bodies cannot function without oxygen. They fatigue, lose coordination, and their muscles become tense, all of which will seriously impair performing. Taking some deep, rhythmic breaths replenishes the oxygen supply, enabling the body to perform its best.

Breathing also has psychological ramifications. A significant problem with over-intensity is that dancers tend to focus on negative symptoms, such as muscle tension and stomach butterflies. By taking slow, deep breaths, dancers can alleviate some of these symptoms, thereby increasing self-confidence and feelings of well-being. Additionally, concentrating on breathing takes their focus off some of the negative feelings. By reducing over-intensity, dancers feel a greater sense of control over their performance.

Progressive relaxation.   One of the most uncomfortable effects of over-intensity is extreme muscle tension. Tight muscles inhibit coordination and increase the likelihood of injury. Helin (1987) reports that members of the Finnish National Ballet stated that they felt tension prior to and during performances and that muscle tension has caused them to perform poorly. They further said that anxiety and muscle tension was highest during dress rehearsals and first night performances.

A common sight backstage is a dancer who looks like he or she is made of stone. Dancers who are very tense will often try to get their muscles to relax by shaking them, but the tension is so great that this does not often work. A technique that usually does work is *progressive relaxation*—tightening and relaxing major muscle groups.

To illustrate this process, consider Rob, a 24-year-old jazz dancer in his first major show. Fifteen minutes before he went on stage, Rob was very nervous and tense. Yet no matter what he did, he couldn't get himself to relax. Fortunately, the week before, one of the choreographers taught him progressive relaxation. She told him that to relax the muscles he must first do just the opposite, that is, tighten them up. So he tightened each of the four major muscle groups (legs and buttocks, chest and back, arms and shoulders, face and neck) for 5 seconds, relaxed them for 5 seconds, and repeated this, taking a deep breath between each phase of the exercise. Almost immediately, he noticed that his muscles were more relaxed and comfortable, and he went on to a fine performance.

This somewhat counterintuitive approach is effective because our muscles work on what is called an opponent-principle process. Returning to the example of Rob, consider a scale of one to ten representing the extent of intensity, where one is completely relaxed and ten is totally uptight. Rob was at about eight, but he needed to be near four in his intensity to dance his best. By tightening his muscles to a ten, the natural reaction of the muscles was to rebound past eight down to a more relaxed state.

Progressive relaxation is valuable to dancers at two levels. First, dancers are often so accustomed to being tense that they are simply not aware of their level of muscle tension and how it affects their performances. Thus, the process of tightening and relaxing teaches dancers to discriminate between the states of tension and relaxation. By doing so, dancers will be more sensitive to their body's signals, and better able to respond effectively to non-optimal levels of intensity. As with any technique, the muscle awareness and control that develops from progressive relaxation takes practice. Make progressive relaxation a part of class and rehearsal. It can be an especially beneficial part of the cool-down.

Smile.   This final physiological intervention is so simple it is surprising that it is so effective. When dancers' intensity levels are too high, have them smile. This does not mean you have to make them happy or enjoy themselves. Chances are, if they are very nervous they will not be in the mood to smile. Rather, have them raise the sides of their mouths into a physical smile. After all, smiling is a motor skill. We discovered this technique several years ago while working with a young dancer, Teri, who became very angry and frustrated during a rehearsal as she struggled to learn difficult parts of her role. She became so tense that she could not have performed the techniques even if she had wanted to. On a whim, the first author told her to smile. As you can imagine, smiling was the last thing she wanted to do and she expressed feelings to us quite emphatically. However, we persisted and simply to appease us, she formed a big, though forced, smile. We told her to hold it for 60 seconds. Within 30 seconds a remarkable change began to occur. As she held the smile, the tension in her shoulders disappeared, the wrinkle in her brow went away, and her body, which had been hunched and closed, began to rise and open up. Within a minute, all of the tension dissipated. She went on to have a productive rehearsal in which she was able to overcome the earlier difficulties.

 ## Center Stage:
Changing Physiology to Reduce Over-Intensity

Have your dancers

- breathe: take long, slow, deep breaths,
- practice progressive relaxation: tighten and relax muscles,
- smile!: when nervous, just smile.

Why did smiling have such a dramatic effect? As we grow up, we become conditioned to associate smiling with happiness and feeling good. Also, when we smile, blood flow through our brain changes and neurochemicals that have a relaxing effect are released. Finally, much like the walk the walk exercise discussed in chapter 2, it is difficult to think and feel contrary to what our bodies are expressing. It is difficult to be angry, frustrated, and tense when we are smiling.

Center Stage:
Increasing Intensity

Have your dancers do the following:

* Increase physical activity: run, jump, move!
* Stop negative thoughts
* Use high-energy thinking and talking: "I will dance great," "I'm ready to go"
* Repeat high-energy words: "reach," "leap"
* Employ high-energy dance imagery

CONTROLLING UNDER-INTENSITY

Although under-intensity is a less common response to an upcoming performance, since it too may have an inhibiting effect, you should teach your dancers to increase intensity to an optimal level.

Elevating intensity involves increasing physiological activity. The most direct means is to engage in any physical activity that boosts heart rate, breathing, and blood flow. To accomplish this, have your dancers practice common exercises prior to a dance performance, like pliés, relevés, and tendus.

Also, changing dancers' thinking can increase intensity. The first step in this process is to get your dancers to stop let-down thoughts, such as, "I don't want to dance this role" or "I wish I were home." Next, encourage your dancers to engage in high-energy thinking and talking. Statements like, "I can't wait to get on stage," "I'm going to dance great tonight," and "Let's go, I'm ready" will excite your dancers and raise their intensity.

Along with detailed statements, dancers should also develop high-energy key words, such as "soar" and "whirl." These key words, emphatically stated, combined with positive and high-energy body language, like arm pumping, fist clenching, and thigh slapping, will further increase intensity. Finally, dancers can engage in high-energy dance imagery to see themselves performing very well and imagine the excitement of a great performance (see chapter 5 for more on dance imagery).

PREPERFORMANCE ROUTINES

Preperformance routines are an effective way to enhance the consistency and quality of performances. They are an important part of preperformance preparation because they help dancers attain and maintain their optimal level of intensity.

Routines ensure completion of every key aspect of preperformance preparation. Routines enhance familiarity of situations. They decrease the likelihood of unexpected events occurring by giving dancers greater control over preperformance events. They develop consistency of thought, feeling, and action. And they increase feelings of control over the performance environment. As a result, routines raise self-confidence and reduce intensity. An effective preperformance routine, regardless of the importance of the role or the production, will condition your dancers' minds and bodies into thinking and feeling that this is just another performance in which they will dance their best. As Paul Taylor said:

> You psyche yourself up. You eliminate any distracting thoughts from your mind. You do physical work too. I went to the theater very early and did a very thorough warm-up and a rehearsal and put my costume and makeup on and then did another warm-up and timed it all very carefully. I had a set preparatory routine. (Lyle, 1977, p. 120)

Routines vs. Rituals

Dancers often exhibit a substantial amount of superstitions. This rigid adherence to preperformance behavior serves no practical function in performance preparation. Often, dancers develop a series of steps that appear to be routines, but are, in fact, superstitious rituals. Learn to distinguish between the two to assist your dancers in developing effective routines.

The goal of routines is to totally prepare dancers for their performance. As such, everything done in preperformance routines should serve a specific and necessary function. Routines should be flexible and adaptable to unique aspects of each performance situation. In contrast, rituals involve things that do not serve a specific purpose in performance preparation. Rituals are inflexible and *must* be done, or dancers will not believe that they will perform well. Show your dancers that they control their routines, but that rituals control them.

Developing a Preperformance Routine

Though routines are individual in nature, each dancer's preperformance routine should include every element that influences performance:

- Meals
- Physical warm-up
- Costume and makeup
- Role warm-up
- Mental preparation

To personalize elements, meet with your dancers and discuss what they do to prepare themselves for a performance. Each of three stages of a preperformance preparation routine—early morning, midday, and final preparation—has unique and essential tasks that must be accomplished to ensure that dancers are optimally prepared to perform their best.

Early morning routine.   Preperformance preparation begins as soon as dancers wake in the morning. This early morning preparation sets the tone for the day. Before dancers get out of bed, they should use dance imagery (see chapter 5) to rehearse their role in the upcoming performance. Next, they should say the dancer's litany out loud, with energy and feeling. These techniques set the stage for the performance by generating positive feelings and focus.

Physical preparation, in the form of rigorous warm-up before breakfast, is also necessary for optimal readiness. When dancers wake up, their core body temperature is 3 to 5 degrees below normal and it takes up to 5 hours to return to normal. If a dancer gets up at 10 a.m. and an afternoon performance begins at 1 p.m., her body may simply not be ready to perform its best and, as a result, performance will suffer. The morning warm-up may include any exercises that work up a sweat, for example, a vigorous barre. Sweating means the body is warming up and will be ready for the performance.

Meals, which have a direct effect on the physiological readiness of dancers, are an important part of early morning preparation. As a general rule, dancers should avoid heavy, sugary, and difficult to digest foods, for example, pancakes, waffles, and eggs. They should eat foods that are high in carbohydrates, low in sugar, and easily digestible, such as bagels, fruit, and plain cereals. Dancers should also drink extra liquids to avoid dehydration during performance.

Midday routine.   A similar preparation process should be conducted at the performance site, several hours before the performance. Prior to rehearsing their roles, dancers should again use dance imagery to produce the feelings associated with a good performance. Imagery and key words may also be used to focus concentration and to begin moving toward optimal levels of intensity.

Then your dancers should begin their physical rehearsal. Initial warm-up and review of the choreography should be slow and gentle to allow the body to warm. The choreography should then be rehearsed with increasing focus and intensity, aimed at simulating performance conditions. This priming makes it easier for dancers to attain their optimal level of focus and intensity when the performance begins.

Final preparation routine. This last stage ensures that dancers are completely and optimally ready just prior to the performance. Place emphasis on dancers fine-tuning themselves mentally and physically to their optimal state of readiness. Final mental preparation involves dancers using imagery to review roles, repeating key words to narrow and maintain concentration and using intensity-control exercises to reach their optimal intensity level. Final physical preparation includes doing traditional warm-up exercises and reviewing critical parts of each dancer's role. Lastly, make any adjustments to costumes and makeup.

The goal of the three levels of preperformance preparation is to ensure that when the dancers go on stage, they are optimally ready, both mentally and physically, to perform their very best. Once you have established the necessary components of the routine, assist each of your dancers in establishing a personalized preperformance routine that satisfies their individual needs and style (see the Personalized Preperformance Routine worksheet).

Personalized Preperformance Routine

Directions: List the activities, thoughts, feelings, and images that will help you prepare to perform your very best.

Early Morning

    Physical:

    Mental:

Midday

    Physical:

    Mental:

(continued)

Final Preparation

    Costume/Makeup:

    Physical:

    Mental:

 ENCORE

At performance time, intensity becomes the most important factor of performance success because if the body is not optimally prepared, dancers will not be able to perform their best.

Intensity is the level of physiological activity dancers experience prior to a performance. A moderate level of intensity is necessary for optimal performance, but too much or too little intensity will hurt performance.

Not one ideal intensity level exists for every dancer. Some dancers perform best at low intensity; others dance best at high intensity.

High intensity is caused by extreme or inaccurate thinking about the performance situation and unfamiliar, unexpected, or uncontrollable events before or during the performance. High intensity is characterized by muscle tension, breathing difficulty, negative self-talk, loss of coordination, and feelings of fear and dread.

Low intensity is caused by over-confidence, lack of motivation, fatigue, and high ability combined with low role demands. Symptoms of low intensity include feelings of lethargy and low energy, an absence of alertness and interest, and problems narrowing concentration prior to and during a performance.

Assess your dancers' intensity levels when they are dancing well vs. poorly to help them reach their optimal level of intensity.

Lessen over-intensity by building self-confidence, countering inaccurate or extreme thinking, assisting your dancers in objectively assessing upcoming auditions or performances, making unfamiliar situations familiar, planning for unexpected events, and helping dancers focus only on events they can control. Over-intensity can be controlled physiologically with the use of breathing, progressive relaxation, and smiling.

Increase intensity by using exercise to raise physiological activity, stopping negative thinking, increasing high-energy thinking and talking, and engaging in motivating dance imagery.

Preperformance routines are an important way for dancers to reach their optimal level of intensity and to ensure total preparedness for the performance. Routines should include only those things that are necessary for optimal performance.

Routines should consist of specific tasks that will prepare dancers physically, technically, artistically, and mentally for the performance. The three stages of effective preperformance routines include early morning, midday, and final preparation.

4

Concentration

Maybe I could compare it to certain meditational states, or states in which you arrive at a certain concentration and then it's not an effort to do what you are concentrating on doing, because your whole system is flowing in that direction. You're acting almost—I wouldn't say in a state of no-mind, but your system is geared to performing. I think of it as . . . a state in which . . . the centers of the mind are in focus, in operation, and all your motor intelligence is blossoming. (Simone Forti in Banes, 1979, 34-35)

Dress Rehearsal:
Improving Concentration

Joanna is a 15-year-old dancer who is performing in her high school's Christmas production. Though quite talented, in last year's show she worried a lot, became very nervous, missed several entrance cues, and forgot some of her role's choreography. This seemed to stem from difficulties she had concentrating during rehearsal, which took place in the high school's busy gymnasium.

1. What factors contributed to her concentration problems?
2. How would you address her current concentration difficulties in rehearsal and during performances?

Reaching the pinnacle of the performing attitude pyramid, the final significant psychological factor that you must address with your dancers is concentration. Concentration is the final component of the PPEP, fine tuning dancers for their upcoming performance.

Of all the psychological influences that affect performance, concentration may be the least understood. It is typically thought of as the ability to focus narrowly on one thing for a long period of time. However, concentration is a complex variable that requires considerable understanding in order to develop concentration skills to effectively enhance performance.

WHAT IS CONCENTRATION?

Following are some key terms applied to dance to help you fully understand concentration. *Attentional field* comprises all things outside of dancers, such as sights and sounds, and all things inside of them, such as thoughts, feelings, and physical responses that they could focus on at any one time. *Attentional focus*, or *concentration*, involves the ability to focus on particular aspects of the attentional field.

Good concentration can be characterized as focusing only on performance-relevant aspects of the attentional field, that is, only those things that are necessary for dancers to perform their best. Important attentional cues for dancers include other dancers, the stage area, props, the music, and offstage cues. Good concentration also involves not being distracted by irrelevant stimuli, staying focused in the present, and should a distraction occur, refocusing attention quickly.

> One's concentration as a performer must . . . remain centered on the action of which one is a part. For it is in truth only one's own concentration on the imagined reality of the role that can force the audience's attention to that same place. (Rick, 1971/72, p. 55)

Conversely, poor concentration involves dancers focusing on performance-irrelevant aspects of the attentional field, that is, on things that do not help them perform their best. Irrelevant cues might include who is in the audience, a problem at home, or plans for tomorrow. Also, poor concentration involves not only losing focus, but having difficulty reestablishing effective concentration.

Maintaining concentration in your dancers is critical not only during performances, but also in class and during rehearsal. Some of dancers' most common concentration problems include being distracted by external cues, such as activity offstage, and by internal cues, such as negative thoughts and pain, forgetting technical instruction during class, focusing on over-intensity rather than dancing well during performances, and thinking about technique when they should be thinking about artistry.

Concentration development requires dancers to identify potential relevant and irrelevant cues in any class, rehearsal, or performance setting; assess their own concentration style; and then, based on this information, use a variety of concentration techniques to maintain proper focus.

> To me, this acquirement of nervous, physical, and emotional concentration is the one element possessed to the highest degree by the truly great dancers of the world. Its acquirement is the result of discipline, of energy in the deep sense. That is why there are so few great dancers. (Graham, 1974, p. 137)

UNDERSTANDING CONCENTRATION STYLES

Help your dancers recognize their own concentration styles. Two concentration styles predominate, impacting dancers' ability to focus and perform during class, rehearsal, and performance. These two styles present their own unique problems that must be addressed in different ways for dancers to maintain effective concentration.

External Focus

Dancers who have an *external focus* are highly sensitive to external cues. In other words, they are easily distracted by activity in their immediate surroundings. Typically, the busier the environment, the more difficulty these dancers will have during class, rehearsal, or performance. Their ability to learn a new skill, rehearse a new role, or dance that role during a performance is inhibited because they cannot effectively block out external distractions. Distractions take focus away from skills or choreography, impeding the learning process, and interfere with preperformance routines that ensure full preparedness. During performances, externally focused dancers may miss their stage cues, lose their timing with the other dancers, or neglect their artistry.

Internal Focus

Dancers who have an *internal focus* are highly sensitive to internal cues. That is, they are overly aware of their own psychological (negative or irrelevant thoughts), emotional (feelings of anxiety and fear), and physical (pounding heart, tense muscles) activity. If these dancers are left alone, they will tend to become overly internally focused on performance-irrelevant cues to the neglect of important performance-relevant external cues. An internal focus hurts dancers in class, rehearsal, and performance.

ENHANCING CONCENTRATION

As with other psychological factors, concentration is a skill that develops with time and practice. Concentration, like any skill, must also be developed incrementally. Teaching concentration to your dancers begins outside the studio, evolves during classes and rehearsals, and reaches fruition with optimal focus during performances.

Enhancing Concentration Outside the Studio

Your dancers can first learn concentration skills during out-of-studio training, for example, while they are stretching or doing Pilates. The first step in this process is to have them put on their "training face" when they work out. The training face involves being totally focused on the exercise in which they are engaging. This means no talking or looking around, concentrating fully on optimal execution of the exercise. Beginning the development of concentration away from the studio allows dancers to identify performance-relevant and irrelevant cues in a setting with relatively few distractions and also enables them to practice good concentration in a stress-free environment.

Enhancing Concentration During Class and Rehearsal

"It is vital to stress to the dancers at the very outset the importance of working with their full concentration and with an eye toward performance at all rehearsals" (Sande, 1977, p. 6). Concentration is the single most important factor in learning new dance skills, because without effective focus, acquiring skills is not possible. Moreover, without technical mastery of all relevant movements, full development of a dancer's performance potential is not possible.

> The mental effort required to obviate mistakes demands so much concentration that other factors, such as expression, are bound to suffer. Repeated activity becomes automatic and is finally executed with little or no thought, thus freeing the mind for the activities of artistic creation. (H'Doubler, 1968, p. 90)

To illustrate, consider the example of Barbara, a dance mistress in a regional ballet company, and Ellen, a two-year member of the company. Ellen had been struggling during the past two days to master a fouetté turn. Barbara would demonstrate the proper movement and make sure Ellen understood. Ellen would be focused on the movement right up until she began it. But then her focus would shift away from the movement to unrelated things. By not focusing on the correct execution of the movement, Ellen could not perform it correctly and was not able to learn it.

> You are not learning how to do steps. You are learning about control and discipline; both the discipline of force and learning to be focused and to concentrate. I look at it as a wonderfully sensitizing process, because to get it right means that you are paying tremendous attention to detail and to a particular physicality. Your awareness of where you are in space is a tremendous asset. (Harkarvy in Hunt, 1992, pp. 54-55)

Your challenge is to ensure that your dancers maintain focus on the technical correction you have given. Getting them to remember to execute the skill as you have instructed is not an easy task because of the many distractions present during class and rehearsal. So, to develop concentration in your dancers you should a) reduce the number of distractions in the setting, and b) provide dancers with skills to narrow their concentration to the task at hand. Use the Concentration Identification worksheet to determine the performance-relevant and irrelevant cues that affect your dancers.

Concentration Identification

Directions: For each situation in which you dance, indicate the specific factors you could focus on that will either help (performance-relevant) or hurt (performance-irrelevant) your dance.

	External and Internal Concentration Cues	
Situation	Help performance (Performance-relevant)	Hurt performance (Performance-irrelevant)

Class

Physical space
(floor surface, room
size, temperature)

People
(other dancers,
instructors, spectators)

Thoughts
(positive, negative,
irrelevant)

Emotions
(joy, anger, depression,
frustration, no emotions)

Intensity
(high, medium, low)

Rehearsal

Physical space
(stage size, lighting)

People
(audience, stage hands)

Thoughts
(anticipation, dread)

Emotions
(excitement, fear)

Intensity
(nervousness, calm)

Performance

Physical space

People

Thoughts

Emotions

Intensity

Simplify the environment. Reducing distractions in the learning environment makes it easier for dancers to focus on dance. Examine the physical and social environment to determine which aspects of the setting are performance-relevant and which are performance-irrelevant. Then remove the performance-irrelevant aspects. Common studio distractions include observers, people entering and leaving, sounds from outside the studio, unnecessary artwork and furniture, clutter, dancers talking and laughing, and a nonprofessional, casual atmosphere.

Technical key word progression. One reason dancers may often have difficulty focusing on the technical instruction you give them is that it may be too long. Make your technical instruction easily useable by reducing the information down to one or two highly descriptive words that dancers can focus on to remind them of the skill to be practiced. That is, give them an *instruction key word* (see the Instruction Key Word Connection worksheet).

Developing an effective key word to supplement your instruction is as important as the instruction itself. The same key word may not work for every dancer, so you and your dancers should be creative in developing key words that are personally meaningful and descriptive. Also, the key word should be as active as possible, for example, "bend" is a better key word than "knees" because the latter does not indicate specifically what should be done.

To effectively incorporate key words in class use the *technical key word progression*. First repeatedly say the key word out loud to your dancers during the entire execution of the movement; this is called *instructor cueing*. It relieves dancers of having to actively concentrate on the skill because you provide them with the focus to execute the skill.

Once dancers can execute the skill with you cueing them, they can then move to the next phase of the exercise, *self-cueing*. At this point, they repeat the key word out loud as they perform the movement. This serves two pur-

Instruction Key Word Connection

Directions: In the left-hand column, write down some of the most common technical or artistic instructions you provide to your dancers. In the right-hand column, list several key words that could be used by your dancers to focus on the instruction.

Instruction	Key words
1.	
2.	
3.	
4.	
5.	
6.	
7.	
8.	

poses: it blocks out other distractions and consciously narrows the dancers' focus to one useful prompt.

Because dancers are able to better focus on a skill, they will begin to internalize it. The next step is for dancers to say the key word silently to themselves. Because the skill is already being acquired, it now requires less concentration to be performed. The goal of this exercise is to enable dancers to perform a skill without conscious thought.

> The dancer must practice her exercises every day . . . must feel so perfectly at ease so far as technique is concerned that when on stage she need not devote to it a single thought, and may concentrate on expression, upon the feeling which must give life to the dances she is performing. (Pavlova in Sorell, 1971, pp. 137-138)

This exercise may be useful not only in class for skill acquisition, but in learning choreography for a role, and in preparing for a performance. Remember that as dancers move from class to rehearsal to performance, both external and internal distractions commensurately increase. More potentially distracting forces put greater demands on dancers' concentration. Distractions present during a rehearsal but not in class include several roles being rehearsed at the same time, spacing, and timing. Those present during a performance, but not in a class or rehearsal, include artistry, audience response, scenery, lighting, and costumes.

Dance imagery. Another means of improving concentration is to have your dancers engage in dance imagery just prior to performing a skill. Using imagery helps dancers narrow their focus to performance-relevant cues and provides them with an image of the correct execution of the skill. Using dance imagery in a variety of settings is discussed in detail in chapter 5.

Preexercise routines. Just as routines are important for preparation prior to performances, they may also be used to improve concentration during class and rehearsal. Often, dancers hurt the quality of their class and rehearsal time by not concentrating prior to and during exercises and role rehearsal. A common scenario is for a dancer to be talking with a friend or still thinking about the previous exercise and, without any refocusing, begin an exercise. Not concentrating on the task at hand results in poor execution.

Center Stage:
Enhancing Concentration in Class and Rehearsal

As instructor, strive to

- simplify the class environment, and
- use technical key word progression.

Have your dancers

- use dance imagery, and
- develop and follow a preexercise routine.

Helping your dancers develop preexercise routines will ensure proper focus and increase the quality of class and rehearsal time. Dancers should follow several key elements in a preexercise routine. First, before every exercise, dancers should stop talking to others around them. Next, they should focus their eyes on the exercise area. Then, they should rehearse the exercise using dance imagery. Finally, dancers should say or think their key word. This preexercise routine takes only 15 to 20 seconds and should be done prior to every exercise. Following a structured preexercise routine will further teach dancers how to control their concentration, which will benefit them as they move to the performance stage.

Center Stage:
Improving Concentration for Performances

Have your dancers

- simulate performances during rehearsal,
- use intensity control techniques,
- block out sights and sounds by going away from activity if offstage activity is distracting,
- stay around offstage activity to keep focus directed externally if distracted by thoughts and feelings,
- repeat performance key words,
- focus on breathing,
- use dance imagery,
- follow their preperformance routine, and
- focus on process rather than outcome.

Enhancing Concentration Prior to and During Performances

As the performance nears, dancers must deal with a variety of internal and external distractions that could interfere with proper concentration. Fortunately, several other concentration strategies enable dancers to fine-tune their focus for the performance. The goal of the process at this stage is to take the focus away from technique and specific physical actions, and direct concentration to the artistry and the totality of the dance.

> The moment concentration is focused upon the actual physical body, and not the movement, the dance disappears. . . . Only when we give ourselves to what is being presented wholly and unequivocally, neither analyzing nor judging, but intuiting what is going on as a *Gestalt*, separating neither the body from the movement nor the movement from the dance, do we see the form which sustains the illusion. (Sheets, 1966, p. 78)

Simulated performances.   Perhaps the best means of developing concentration for upcoming performances is through simulated performances, such as final dress rehearsal and preopening performances, and with the use of dance imagery. Being able to dance or imagine dancing in a realistic performance setting has several benefits. It enables dancers to identify performance-relevant and irrelevant cues. It also shows them how the setting affects their individual concentration style. Finally, it provides them the opportunity to develop situation-specific strategies to maintain their performance focus.

Performance key words. When performance time arrives, numerous distractions may impair concentration and hurt performance. *Performance key words* can be used to block out distractions and narrow focus. Common performance key words include "reach," "feel," and "project." They may also be used to refocus if concentration is disturbed. In assisting your dancers to develop useful performance key words, keep the following in mind. Key words should be positive, based in the present, and related to the process instead of the outcome (see the Performance Key Words worksheet).

Intensity control. Evidence suggests that dancers' intensity levels have a significant influence on concentration. Most notable, increased intensity narrows concentration and lessens the ability to shift focus. Decreased intensity

---

Performance Key Words

Directions: The key words below may be used to maintain confidence, control intensity, enhance artistry, and improve overall concentration. List some of your own meaningful key words that enable you to focus on an important aspect of your performance.

Breathe	Relax
Loose	Trust
Go for it	Do it
Calm	Feel
Reach	Positive
Focus	Commit

results in being unable to narrow focus to performance cues. Consequently, the intensity control techniques described in chapter 3, including breathing and progressive relaxation, will also help dancers maintain effective concentration.

Concentration techniques for performances. As discussed, two predominant concentration styles present some unique problems for dancers preparing to perform. Once you have helped your dancers identify their personal concentration styles, either internal or external, show them how to best structure their preperformance environment so they will be properly focused when they go on stage. To illustrate, consider the examples of two professional jazz dancers, Debbie and Carl, who have contrasting concentration styles. Here's how they were able to control their concentration to perform their best.

Debbie has an external focus, which, as mentioned, means that she is easily distracted by the activity around the theater prior to and during a performance. Her concentration goal was to block out the external distractions that interfere with her preperformance preparation. Most dancers process the world through sight and sound, so they will become distracted by external visual and auditory activity. Debbie needed to take steps to minimize these two particular types of distractions. She improved her concentration by managing her immediate environment. Because of her external focus, the worst thing she could do was to stay in the offstage areas busy with many people and considerable activity. Before her performance and during offstage show time, she went off by herself where there were few external distractions. Separated from the offstage activity, she focused on her preperformance routine, which increased her overall concentration.

She also learned to control her eyes to avoid looking at potential distractions and she listened to her personal stereo as she went through her preperformance routine to keep out distracting noise. Finally, just prior to going on-stage, she used some intensity-control techniques and repeated her performance key word, providing ideal focus and intensity.

In contrast to Debbie, Carl became overwhelmed by his own internal activity. He worried about how he would perform and about his symptoms of over-intensity. His concentration goal was to block out internal distractions, that is, stop himself from thinking about unnecessary things, and reduce his over-intensity so it would not be distracting.

Carl also improved his concentration by managing his environment. However, unlike Debbie, the worst thing he could do was go off by himself away from the activity. This would only give him the opportunity to stay internally focused on things that would hurt his preparation. Rather, the offstage activity drew his focus externally and prevented him from thinking too much. So Carl went through his preperformance routine around other dancers, keeping himself occupied with conversation and watching the activity.

Carl listened to his personal stereo, which focused his attention on enjoyable music rather than on his negative thoughts. Also, to reduce the internal distractions of his over-intensity, Carl used intensity-control techniques to remove the symptoms. Finally, as his time on-stage approached, he rehearsed his performance using imagery and repeated his performance key word, which also decreased unnecessary thinking and improved his concentration.

Concentration Problems and Solutions During a Performance

As mentioned, once the performance begins, concentration dictates the quality of the performance. Some concentration problems arise prior to and during a performance that are common to most dancers and to most performance settings. Following are typical problems and solutions to them that dancers may use to maintain their performance focus.

Delay in the start of a performance.   Delays due to technical difficulties, a late arriving audience, and last minute program changes may be disruptive to dancers who have been preparing themselves to begin at a certain time. These delays may either produce over-intensity due to unexpectedness or under-intensity due to the letdown of not being able to begin. Most often, dancers will just stand around, letting the delay rattle them and losing their focus.

Provide your dancers with skills to respond effectively to a delay, so they will be ready when the performance finally begins. When a delay occurs, dancers should take steps to maintain their physical and mental preparedness. First, they should repeat their preperformance routines. This alone will keep them focused on the upcoming performance, help them maintain their optimal intensity, and reduce the likelihood of the delay negatively affecting them. Also, they can rehearse critical parts of their choreography to maintain their self-confidence. If there is insufficient space to physically rehearse, dancers should use dance imagery to review their role. Finally, they should repeat their performance key words to block out interfering thoughts.

Mistake during the performance.   Dancers do not always dance a flawless performance from start to finish. Because of distractions, poor intensity, or other reasons, they may make a mistake. Unfortunately, it is not uncommon for one mistake to hurt their entire performance. Show your dancers how they can reestablish their form and give a strong performance for the remainder of the show.

When dancers make a mistake, they have two typical responses. First, their focus shifts from performance-relevant cues to the difficulties they are having. Second, they worry and their intensity increases. This in turn causes their performance to deteriorate even more. Their goal must be to reestablish focus and maintain optimal intensity.

The first thing dancers need to do is to regain their concentration. This can be accomplished by having a predetermined performance key word to silently repeat to draw their focus back to the choreography and away from the difficulties. Next, to decrease the likelihood of over-intensity, dancers should take long, slow, deep breaths. The breathing will produce a relaxing effect and also act as a focusing technique.

Offstage, dancers can use intensity-control techniques to further maintain optimal intensity. Additionally, they can use dance imagery to instill a positive and successful image and feeling for the remainder of the performance.

External and internal distractions.   Distractions, both internal and external, are also present on-stage. These may include the audience, offstage activity, other dancers, irrelevant thoughts, and fatigue. When dancers are distracted, they must refocus their attention in order to maintain a quality performance.

For external distractions, dancers can repeat their performance key word. This pulls their concentration inward, away from the external activity. They can also control their eyes and narrow their visual focus to more performance-relevant cues, such as the stage, the set, or other dancers with whom they are interacting.

For internal distractions, dancers can also repeat their performance key word. This will block out unnecessary thoughts and feelings. They can also redirect their focus outward, to the stage, other dancers, or the surroundings.

Process vs. outcome focus.   Dancers have a tendency to look ahead to the completion of a successful performance and the accolades they will receive. This focus on outcome will often cause mistakes in the performance, for psychological and physical reasons. It draws dancers' concentration away from things they need to focus on in order to dance well. Also, thinking about the end of the performance decreases intensity, so dancers are not physically capable of performing well. Dancers must bring their concentration back to the process, that is, focus on performance-relevant cues.

By repeating performance key words, dancers can bring their focus back to the present and to cues that will enable them to perform their best. Also, they can concentrate outwardly on the other dancers and the current choreography. Finally, in order to maintain optimal intensity, they can use motivating self-talk such as "keep at it" or "strive."

 ENCORE

Concentration is typically, and incorrectly, considered the ability to focus intently on one thing for an extended period of time. In fact, concentration is a complex variable that is influenced by both psychological and environmental factors.

Attentional field is everything inside and outside of dancers that they could focus on at any one time. Good concentration involves focusing on performance-relevant aspects of the attentional field, such as the choreography, other dancers, and offstage cues. Bad concentration involves focusing on performance-irrelevant aspects of the attentional field such as who is in the audience or what kind of reviews dancers will receive after the performance.

Maintaining good concentration is important in class, rehearsal, and during performances. Common concentration problems include being distracted by external cues, such as activity offstage, or by internal cues, such as negative thoughts and pain; forgetting technical instruction during class; focusing on over-intensity rather than on dancing well during performances; and thinking about technique when they should be thinking about artistry.

Two types of concentration styles are most common among dancers: External focus, in which they are sensitive to and distracted by environmental activity, such as the audience and other dancers, and internal focus, in which they are sensitive to and distracted by intrapersonal activity, such as thoughts and physical sensations.

Concentration is critical during class because without proper focus learning cannot occur. Concentration during class is often lost because internal and external distractions draw focus away from instruction.

A technical key word is a word that summarizes your instructional feedback and reminds dancers of the skill to work on. Key word progression allows dancers to maintain their concentration, enabling them to progressively learn new skills.

Dance imagery and preexercise routines are also effective means for improving concentration during class and rehearsal.

During performances, dancers who are externally focused can block out environmental distractions by avoiding offstage activity, controlling their eyes, repeating their key words, and using intensity-control techniques. Dancers who are internally focused can block out unnecessary thoughts and feelings by staying amid offstage activity, talking to other dancers, focusing on their preperformance routines, and using dance imagery.

Common problems occur during performances, such as delays, mistakes, external and internal distractions, and focusing on outcome rather than process. They disrupt concentration and need to be addressed in order for dancers to perform their best.

To regain their concentration when focus is lost due to these distractions, dancers should repeat performance key words, use intensity-control techniques, control their eyes, and focus on the current choreography.

5

Dance Imagery

In using imagery I try to compress the material in such a way that I can get as many levels into one image as can be packed into it. I try to make each image as evocative as I can, on as many levels as possible, so that a person can hook into one level or another, or more than one. It is like a mosaic with bits of information which can be put together in different ways so that each person comes away with something individually meaningful. (Meredith Monk in Kreemer, 1987, p. 254)

Dress Rehearsal:
Using Dance Imagery

Cameron is a 26-year-old modern dancer with a small regional company. Shy by nature and quite uncomfortable performing in front of a large audience, he is often unable to fully express himself in his role. This discomfort hurts his confidence and his ability to concentrate.

1. How would dance imagery help Cameron overcome his discomfort?
2. What goals could Cameron set using dance imagery?
3. Where could Cameron use dance imagery to gain the greatest benefits?

A common sight backstage at performances is dancers with their eyes closed, slowly rehearsing the critical elements of their roles. They are imagining themselves performing with mastery and virtuosity. They are envisioning the proper execution of their movements and, most importantly, feeling the artistry of their role. As Tommy Tune once said, "I dance images in my head . . . I like to get an image in my head of something . . . the slow gait of a five-gaited horse, a giraffe running over a plain, a rubber band being stretched—and I let the image work through the rest of my body" (Ellfeldt, 1976, p. 205).

Mental imagery is used by great performers in a variety of fields. It can improve self-confidence, control intensity, increase concentration, and facilitate skill acquisition. Additionally, Hanrahan and Salmela (1990) found that dancers use mental imagery at or away from the studio to enhance the quality of training. It may also be used during the off-season to further develop dancers' performances.

Dance imagery is one of the most powerful tools available to you and your dancers and is used extensively in the PPEP. "Visualization, mind's eye, imagery . . . they hold the potential for the dancer, teacher, and choreographer in their capacity to enhance learning skills and performance" (Smith, 1990). Yet for all of its benefits, it is not often fully understood. Dance imagery refers to repeatedly envisioning a dance performance, with the goal of improving some aspect of the performance—technical (turns or jumps), psychological (self-confidence or motivation), or physiological (intensity). Furthermore, it is rarely used in a manner that optimizes its value. For dance imagery to be most useful, dancers must develop and implement a systematic program in which dance imagery is incorporated into class and rehearsal time, preperformance preparation, and out-of-studio training. As seen in previous chapters, dance imagery can enhance motivation, self-confidence, intensity, and concentration. This chapter provides a full explanation of dance imagery and how it can be used to increase the quality of your dancers' experience.

UNDERSTANDING DANCE IMAGERY

In order to teach your dancers how to develop an effective dance imagery program, some essential factors must be understood. Each of the following techniques maximizes the quality of mental imagery.

Imagining Total Performance

Many dancers call dance imagery visualization, because they have the misconception that it mainly involves seeing the performance. However, quality dance imagery involves total reproduction of all aspects of performance, including physiological and psychological experiences. The *visual* component consists of anything that your dancers see during a performance, such as the stage area, props, and other dancers. The *auditory* element involves everything your dancers hear during a performance, including music and offstage cues. The *kinesthetic* aspects include muscular sensations, heartbeat, and breathing. The *thinking* components comprise thoughts and images that occur during a performance. Finally, the *emotional* elements include feelings of excitement, frustration, joy, and fear. Thus, dance imagery is more than just mental rehearsal. Just as your dancers become absorbed in the actual dance experience, so too should they be with effective dance imagery.

Imagery Perspective

Dance imagery can take two views: internal and external. An *internal perspective* refers to dancers seeing the imagined performance through their own eyes, as if they were actually performing. An *external perspective* involves dancers seeing the imagined performance from outside their body, as if they were watching the performance on video. It was initially believed that the internal perspective was better for several reasons. First, it would be easier to imagine the total performance because the diverse components are experienced internally. Second, since the perspective during actual performance is internal, the internal imagery perspective should be more realistic and easier to create. Third, since dancers actually perform from an internal perspective, using external imagery involves a frame of reference that is unfamiliar. In fact, early research reported that successful performers were more likely to use internal imagery than less successful performers and that internal imagery resulted in more vivid images and better performance than external imagery.

However, other research has demonstrated no differences in imagery quality or performance between perspectives. Also, it appears that some dancers are naturally internal imagers and others are external imagers. Dancers should rely on the style that is most natural to them, but also experiment with the other style.

Imagery perspectives may have differential benefits depending on what is being worked on with the imagery. Specifically, external imagery may be better when dancers are first learning new skills. In the early stages of learning, dancers may lack physical kinesthetic awareness in their internal imagery to ensure that their bodies are positioned correctly and that they are executing the skill properly. By using external imagery, dancers can see if they are performing the skill accurately; much like watching a videotape to critique technique. Once the basics of the skill have been learned, dancers must internalize the feeling of the skill. At this point, they may switch to internal imagery to facilitate this process.

Vivid Imagery

Vivid images are realistic, detailed, and clear and include all of the requisite senses, thoughts, and emotions. Vivid images replicate actual experience, increasing the likelihood of proper performance in the future. In fact, highly skilled performers report more vivid imagery. "When the final image is clearly and vividly sensed, it demands release and tends to expel itself from the mind . . . and find expression in movement" (H'Doubler, 1968, p. 118).

Imagery is a skill that improves with practice, not an inborn quality that dancers either have or do not have. Dancers often say that they cannot imagine or that their imagery is fuzzy and unclear. Unclear imagery may be due to underdeveloped imagery skills or lack of familiarity with the images of dance. In other words, some dancers may be able to vividly imagine scenes that are familiar to them, such as the feel of walking on a beach, but be less able to imagine themselves executing a double turn.

To determine whether dancers need either to develop imagery skills or familiarity with dance images, use a simple test. First, have your dancers imagine a very familiar object such as an orange. (See if they imagine the sight, feel, smell, and taste of an orange.) Next, ask them to imagine themselves executing some basic techniques, such as a pirouette. Then, have them imagine themselves performing a role in a production. If there is a decline in vividness from the orange to the technique to the dance performance, you can assume their imagery skills are sound, but they need to work on applying those skills to their dance.

Dance imagery skills can be improved in several ways. Some dancers have difficulty imagining themselves performing if they have never seen themselves dance. By viewing videos of themselves, they can internalize the video image of their own unique style, and by watching better dancers, they can see what improvements they need to make. Also, during class and rehearsal, they should take time to imagine recently executed skills. This facilitates the imagery process by generating images while associated feelings are fresh in their minds and bodies.

However, if dancers have difficulty imagining the three scenes at all, then they need to learn basic imagery skills. Have them use the exercises just described, and take time away from the studio to practice the following series of exercises that will enhance their fundamental imagery skills. The objective of these exercises is for dancers to practice reproducing various elements of good imagery. Each day, dancers should choose one aspect of imagery, for example, visual, sensory, or kinesthetic, and a familiar object to represent it, then focus on reproducing a clearly mental picture of that element. In time, each of these components will become more vivid. Once clarity has been achieved, the exercise should be repeated using a familiar dance situation, then a less familiar one. Increased imagery vividness will eventually generalize to more unfamiliar and complex situations, developing a sound, basic level of imagery skill.

Once your dancers have developed imagery skills, you can facilitate the clarity of imagery by providing them with images. "One of the functions of your dance teacher is to provide images that you can apply to your dancing. Some teachers are better at suggesting them than others, and there are a few you'll find who will give you vivid pictures that will work like magic to enable you to improve your dancing" (Loren, 1978, p. 206). Images can be many types. You can use another dancer, either in person or on video. You may use metaphors, for example, "Feel like a swan flying across the stage." In fact, you can use images involving any of the senses, emotions, or physical sensations. Also, because one image may not work for all dancers, provide individualized images. With experience, and fuller understanding of your dancers, you will become more skilled at providing just the right image that will work with each dancer.

Imagery Control

Dancers' most common concern when they do imagery is that they see themselves making mistakes. This causes frustration and doubt in their ability. This concern is critical because dance imagery is similar to actual physical practice. In actual practice, if dancers rehearse a skill incorrectly, they will internalize its improper execution, that is, they will become very good at doing the wrong thing. The same holds true with imagery. Imagining incorrect skills will result in incorrect images being ingrained. To successfully manipulate their images, dancers need to learn *imagery control*. Also uncontrollable images produce distractions, which further hurt imagery. Being able to control imagery increases self-confidence and expectations for future success. Consequently, it is essential for your dancers to produce only positive, successful images. As with imagery vividness, imagery control is a skill that develops with time. Educate your dancers about this, because poor imagery control may discourage them from putting in the time and effort necessary to improve their imagery skills.

Invariably, in the early stages of a dance imagery program, your dancers will struggle with some poor imagery control. This lack of control will manifest itself in technical mistakes, spontaneous negative thoughts, and difficulties focusing during the imagery. It is critical that your dancers do not let these unsuccessful or negative images go by without modification. Poor dance imagery inhibits the development process in two ways. First, every time dancers produce a poor image, they do not learn from an effective image. Second, the poor image becomes internalized, making it harder to learn effective images and more difficult to change poor ones.

When dancers engage in poor imagery, they must immediately correct it with better imagery. Think of dance imagery as a film running through your dancers' heads. When dancers make a mistake, they should rewind the film and "edit" the imagery until they are able to imagine the scene correctly. Following is an exercise to help this imagery editing process.

It can be difficult to learn a new technique at full speed. So actual practice of a skill is often broken down into component parts and each part is executed in slow motion. The same approach can be taken with dance imagery. If your dancers are unable to imagine a skill or sequence of movements correctly at full speed, have them slow the "film" down (frame by frame, if necessary), and imagine themselves performing each part of the skill or sequence correctly. Once able to imagine it in slow motion, they can progressively speed up the imagery until they can perform the skill at normal speed. This exercise enables dancers to learn effective imagery control in a short time. Once control is established, future imagery remains controlled and mistake-free.

Combine Relaxation With Imagery

Dance imagery can also be facilitated by preceding it with some relaxation exercises. Increased intensity can hurt concentration and disturb the integrity of the image. Inducing a relaxed state results in greater imagery vividness and control. Additionally, a relaxed state may make dancers more open to imagined scenes. Dancers can use the progressive relaxation procedure described in chapter 3 to produce a relaxed condition prior to imagery.

Imagine Realistic Conditions

A benefit of using dance imagery is that it enables dancers to perform in a situation many times before they actually do. Also, it allows them to adapt to any unusual or uncomfortable aspects of the performance setting. For the greatest benefits then, dancers should imagine themselves performing under realistic conditions. For example, if your company will be dancing on a stage that is uneven and slippery, have them imagine themselves adjusting to and performing well under these conditions. Dancers have a tendency to want to perform under ideal conditions and may, as a result, imagine themselves dancing in a problem-free setting. Unless they are assured of performing under perfect conditions they should not imagine themselves doing so. Dancers should always engage in dance imagery using the conditions in which they are most likely to perform.

Imagine Realistic Performances

As dancers develop, they will learn more difficult skills and perform more challenging roles. As they adjust to the demands of each new level, they will not perform flawlessly right away; there will initially be some mistakes. Consequently, when your dancers imagine themselves performing a new skill or role, they should not imagine themselves performing perfectly. They should not see themselves performing like a premier danseur (unless they are one). Instead, they should imagine themselves performing within their ability and coping well with the new demands.

Adjust Imagery Speed

As mentioned, using slow-motion imagery can help dancers overcome mistakes in their imagery. It can also be used to learn new skills. By slowing imagery down, dancers are better able to focus on particular components, leading to mastery. Imagery may then be speeded up and artistry incorporated to further internalize the movement.

Fast-motion imagery is beneficial to dancers in order to focus on speed and reaction. Just as in actual practice and performance, thoughts and external distractions can interfere with performance. Similarly, using dance imagery, thoughts can intrude, diminishing concentration and interrupting imagined performance. Dancers can learn to avoid these intrusions with fast-motion imagery. By speeding up imagery, dancers become more focused on the performance and do not have time to be distracted by thoughts and external factors. This process also increases reliance on internalized habits and artistry.

Feel the Imagery

As discussed, effective dance imagery is more than just visual. In fact, it's vital that dancers *feel* it in their bodies. This should be a fundamental goal of all dance imagery. To increase feeling in imagery, combine imagined and real sensations. Have your dancers move their bodies with their imagery to simulate actual movement.

Not Feeling Right

It is not uncommon for dancers to begin class, rehearsal, or a performance not feeling good about their dancing. They may say they are a little tight, their timing is off, or they just don't feel like they are dancing well. Moreover, no matter how much they try to warm up, they just can't seem to get that good feeling. If the problem is mental, and the dancers are physically fine, but do not believe they are, they will lose self-confidence and become over-intense and distracted. If it is physical, such as fatigue or illness, they will be unable to perform well.

 Center Stage:
Understanding Dance Imagery

Have your dancers

- imagine total performance,
- experiment with internal and external perspectives,
- increase vividness and control,
- combine relaxation with imagery,
- imagine realistic conditions and performances,
- adjust imagery speed,
- feel the imagery, and
- use imagery to establish good feelings.

Dance imagery can be used to reestablish the good feeling that will enable them to perform as well as they can. Have your dancers imagine a past performance in which they felt great and performed very well. Then they should reproduce the thoughts, emotions, and physical feelings of that performance and bring them forward to the present. This process generates confidence and positive emotions, and activates the body toward optimal intensity.

WHEN TO USE DANCE IMAGERY

Dance imagery is a tool that may be used in a variety of settings to enhance the quality of training and preperformance preparation. For dancers to benefit from this technique, dance imagery must be made a regular and consistent part of your dancers' training regimen.

During Class and Rehearsal

Dance imagery facilitates learning when incorporated into several phases of class and rehearsal. "In a learning situation the use of imagery can improve communication between teacher and student. . . . A teacher with an arsenal of images has the ability to find a concise way of describing a movement" (Smith, 1990, p. 17). After dancers complete an exercise or some choreography for a role, assess the outcome. If dancers performed well, you want them to remember what it felt like to perform that way. So have them immediately reproduce the performance in their imagery. If they performed poorly, have them immediately imagine the performance, but this time doing it correctly. This "cleanses" the muscles of the memory of the poor performance and replaces it with a correct feeling.

Also, after an exercise or role rehearsal, teachers often give dancers some instructional feedback. Unfortunately, dancers often forget or do not pay attention to that instruction when they again begin the exercise or choreography. Instead of simply asking them if they understand the instruction, have them use dance imagery to help the retention process. Have dancers close their eyes and immediately imagine themselves executing the skill, but this time with the corrections you have provided. This causes them to focus on the performance and produces an image and feeling that will serve them well when they perform the skill or role again.

During class and rehearsal, dancers often stand around waiting for their turn to perform. While standing idle, they will typically talk among themselves, which takes their minds off the class or rehearsal. Replace this inefficient period with dance imagery. Instruct your dancers to review with imagery what they just learned and to imagine themselves performing correctly the next time they dance.

Finally, as described in chapter 4, dance imagery can be part of a preexercise routine. "A technique for using mental rehearsal during class that you might find effective is to flash an image across your mental screen a split second before you're about to do the movement" (Loren, 1978, p. 216). When dancers engage in dance imagery, they are focusing on their dance and generating a positive and successful image with which to begin the exercise. Using effective concentration and an appropriate image, it is more likely that your dancers will perform each exercise or piece of choreography properly, enhancing learning and performance quality.

Preperformance Preparation

Though preperformance routines usually start the morning of a performance, dance imagery can be used to initiate performance preparation the week prior to opening night. As mentioned, a significant cause of confidence, intensity, and concentration problems before a performance is lack of experience or familiarity with the performance setting. Dance imagery can lessen some of these difficulties by allowing dancers to mentally perform at the site several times before opening night. This enables dancers to familiarize themselves with the entire performance scenario, rehearse their roles, practice coping strategies to deal with distractions, and build confidence through successful performance. When opening night arrives, dancers will feel that they have already performed several times, and are more likely to be confident, relaxed, and focused. In addition, as discussed in chapter 3, dance imagery should be included in all aspects of dancers' preperformance routines on the day of the performance.

DEVELOPING A DANCE IMAGERY PROGRAM

Imagery can also be valuable as part of the PPEP that your dancers engage in on their own away from the studio. To illustrate the value of a dance imagery program, consider how such a program helped a 25-year-old dancer, Todd, who dances in a local jazz company, to improve his performances.

Setting Dance Imagery Goals

Whenever using imagery, dancers should have goals and purposes. These goals are much like the micro goals recommended in chapter 1. Each time your dancers use imagery, they should know exactly what they want to focus on and how they will accomplish it.

Have your dancers decide in which areas they want to work. Three primary areas on which dancers may focus their imagery include: technical, psychological, and performance. *Technical* includes mastering new skills, practicing a new sequence of movements, or rehearsing a new role. *Psychological* consists of developing a psychological skill, such as self-confidence, intensity, concentration, or motivation. *Performance* relates to improving overall performance, for example, developing consistency or enhancing the artistry of a role. Using the Dance Imagery Goals worksheet, have your dancers list what they want to individually work on. Your dancers can set several goals, but they should only work on one goal at a time. When one goal has been reached, they can then move on to the next one. This way, dancers are able to put their full focus and energy into each goal until it is achieved, enabling them to more quickly and easily accomplish the subsequent goals.

Todd had two dance imagery goals. First he wanted to be more relaxed before going on-stage. Second, Todd wanted to go beyond the technical execution of his roles and add artistry and energy to his dance.

Climbing the Dance Imagery Ladder

Developing skills with a dance imagery program involves an incremental process in which dancers imagine themselves dancing in more and more

---

Dance Imagery Goals

Directions: In the space below, indicate your goals for the dance imagery program. Be specific in identifying areas where you want to improve.

Technical goals:

Psychological goals:

Performance goals:

---

difficult situations. It would not be realistic for your dancers to begin their dance imagery program by imagining themselves performing a difficult role. Just as dancers develop increasingly more challenging skills and master new roles in actual performance, a similar approach should be used in their dance imagery. Consequently, your dancers should create a ladder of class, rehearsal, and performance situations in which they can imagine themselves (see the Dance Imagery Ladder worksheet). The ladder should start with the least important situation in which your dancers would be working on their imagery goal, for example, working on a new sequence of movements alone in the studio. Once the imagery goal at the first rung of the ladder has been achieved mentally and actually, your dancers may then progress to the next rung. This process continues until dancers are able to imagine themselves accomplishing their imagery goal in the most important dance situation they will perform, for example, opening night.

Patience is an important attribute in dance imagery because you do not want your dancers rushing up the dance imagery ladder. Rather, they should

---

Dance Imagery Ladder

Directions: In the space below, create a ladder of class, rehearsal, and performance situations in which you will imagine yourself. The ladder should increase incrementally in importance.

Least important

    1.

    2.

Moderately important

    3.

    4.

Most important

    5.

---

take their time at each rung. Once the imagery goal has been reached for the first time at a particular rung, dancers should stay there for several sessions to fully internalize the situation and reinforce the positive images, thoughts, and feelings.

Todd established a dance imagery ladder that began with him rehearsing his role in an upcoming production alone in the studio. In his imagery, Todd rehearsed the technical aspects of his role until he had learned it so well he could then add artistry and energy. Also, prior to each imagined run-through, he physically practiced several relaxation techniques including deep breathing and progressive relaxation. He was able to work on both of his imagery goals at once, because rather than interfering with each other, his first goal of learning to relax facilitated his second goal of incorporating more artistry and energy into his performances. After a few more sessions repeating this imagery, he moved up to the next rung, which involved rehearsing his role privately with the dance instructor. Subsequent rungs included working on his goals in an organized rehearsal several weeks prior to opening night at a rehearsal in the auditorium where the performance would be held, in a final dress rehearsal, and, lastly, performing on opening night. By opening night, Todd was able to perform his role in his dance imagery and actual rehearsals with artistry and energy.

Center Stage:
Developing a Dance Imagery Program

Have your dancers do the following:

- Set imagery goals.
- Climb the dance imagery ladder.
- Practice situation-specific imagery.
- Hold regular imagery sessions: Each session should last about 10 minutes, and sessions should take place three to four times a week.
- Keep a dance imagery journal: They can record imagery sessions (performance, thoughts, feelings, problems), and track progress over time.
- Use imagery: They can incorporate it into an overall training program as part of in-studio training (after feedback, before next exercise, to prepare for the next performance, the day of a performance).
- Learn patience: With diligence, dancers can expect to see results in 6 to 8 weeks.

Situation-Specific Dance Imagery

Dancers will often imagine themselves performing in an unspecified performance at an undetermined site. This lack of specificity limits the value of the imagery because dancers are not able to respond to the environmental, social, and situational cues present during an actual performance.

Consequently, when your dancers develop a dance imagery program, they should be sure that each session takes place in the context of a specific class, performance, role, studio, or production site. In other words, dancers should imagine themselves dancing in particular situations. To increase their ability to adapt to changing settings, dancers can select slightly different situations within each rung of the dance imagery ladder. Dancers should be sure to imagine themselves performing in situations that are appropriate to their level of ability. For example, if a dancer is a member of a regional modern dance company, she should not imagine herself performing at Lincoln Center.

Imagery Sessions

Dancers should structure their imagery sessions to maximize their value. They should be encouraged to set aside a specific time each day to practice imagery sessions. If the sessions are a regular part of their daily routine, dancers are more likely to adhere to the program.

Your dancers should also have a quiet and comfortable place where they will not be disturbed. Some studios set aside a room where dancers may go after class or rehearsal to work on their imagery.

Dance imagery should be done three to four times a week. Your most highly motivated dancers may want to do imagery every day, but overuse should be discouraged, because like any form of training, too much can lead to burnout and a loss of desire to continue.

Finally, imagery sessions should last no longer than 10 minutes. Keeping the sessions brief increases motivation, decreases boredom, and ensures consistent concentration throughout the session.

Dance Imagery Journal

A difficulty with dance imagery is that the results are not immediate or tangible. Unlike other forms of training, such as stretching or Pilates, the benefits of dance imagery, such as increased self-confidence or improved concentration, cannot be clearly measured. As discussed in chapter 1, it is motivating to see improvement over time. To track results of dance imagery, dancers should keep a *dance imagery journal.* The purpose of a dance imagery journal is to record every imagery session, enabling dancers to more clearly

Dance Imagery Journal

Date	Site	Type	Quality	Thoughts and Feelings	Improvement	Future work
June 16	*Auditorium*	*Dress rehearsal*	*Consistent Lacked artistry*	*Negative thoughts; used thought-stopping. Felt tense; used breathing, smile, progressive relaxation.*	*Had few negative thoughts; more controlled imagery.*	*Focus on relaxation, confidence, artistry.*

see improvement in their imagined performances. The Dance Imagery Journal worksheet lists information that should be included: date, site, type and quality of the performance, related thoughts and feelings, improvements over previous sessions, and areas for future work. This information could also be incorporated into dancers' daily dance diary.

Dance Imagery Expectations

Some dancers believe that they will receive immediate benefits from dance imagery. However, as with any type of training, this expectation is unrealistic. Dancers should understand the need for consistent adherence to the program and patience in looking for results. Relate this to the time and effort needed to benefit from technical or physical training. If dancers diligently follow their dance imagery program, they can expect to see results within six to eight weeks.

Learn More About Imagery

If you are interested in learning other ways to improve imagery in your dancers, read the book *Put Your Mother on the Ceiling*, by Richard deMille (1981). It consists of many fun and interesting exercises to develop a variety of imagery skills, including vividness, control, perspective, and total reproduction.

 ENCORE

Dance imagery is one of the most powerful tools available to you and your dancers. Imagery can improve psychological skills, such as self-confidence and concentration, facilitate skill acquisition, and enhance performance preparation.

Dance imagery refers to repeatedly envisioning a dance performance with the goal of improving some aspect of the performance.

The following factors optimize the benefits of dance imagery: imagining total performance (all senses, thoughts, emotions, and physical feelings), using either an internal or external perspective, and developing vivid and controlled images.

Other factors that influence the quality of dance imagery include combining relaxation with imagery, imagining realistic conditions and performances, adjusting imagery speed for different purposes, and emphasizing the feeling aspects of imagery.

Dance imagery can enhance the quality of class and rehearsal time by improving concentration and producing positive and successful images of what dancers are working on.

Dance imagery improves preperformance preparation by allowing dancers to perform, in their mind's eye, many times before the actual performance, enabling them to be more confident, relaxed, and focused.

To develop and implement an effective dance imagery program, dancers must set dance imagery goals and establish a dance imagery ladder. Imagery sessions should last no longer than 10 minutes, be situation-specific, occur no more than three to four times a week, and be done in a quiet, comfortable place where dancers will not be disturbed.

Dancers should have realistic expectations about the dance imagery program. They must realize that, like any type of training, results will come with time and effort. They can expect to see benefits within six to eight weeks.

6

Slumps, Stress, and Burnout

If you find yourself not making any progress for a while, don't despair. . . . Becoming worried and frantic won't help either. Simply recognize that you've run into an obstacle. . . . Then develop a plan to help yourself around it. . . . Keep calm as you follow your plan. . . . Stay attuned to your bodily sensations, invite encouragement of friends, and continue to maintain respect for yourself as a dancer and a person. (Loren, 1978, pp. 195-196)

Dress Rehearsal:
Overcoming a Performance Slump

Erica is a 28-year-old ballet dancer with a small regional company. As their prima ballerina and most experienced dancer, she is given most of the demanding lead roles and also assists the artistic director and dance mistress with choreography, classes, and rehearsals. Erica also teaches at a local dance studio three nights a week to make ends meet. For the last month, her dancing has been inconsistent and full of mistakes, she has lacked the energy and focus for which she is known, and she has lost some of her confidence.

1. What do you see as the primary cause of her performance slump? What are some of the contributing causes to the slump?

2. What should be the primary focus of a slumpbusting plan to alleviate her slump? What specific components should be included in the slumpbusting plan?

Slumps, extreme drops in performance, are an inevitable and natural part of being a dancer. They are also a continuous source of concern, confusion, and frustration for you and your dancers. Moreover, dancers seem to fall into slumps and come out of them for no apparent reason. No one agrees on what causes slumps. Some dance professionals attribute a dramatic drop in performance to psychological causes, whereas others think it is purely physical. Also, no one agrees on how to cure slumps. Some believe that dancers should increase their training and work through it. Others suggest the opposite: totally abstaining from training and performance for a period, when possible.

Whatever viewpoint is held, the fact is that slumps do pass and, with time, performance will return to its normal level. Unfortunately, dancers do not often have the luxury of waiting for slumps to pass. With upcoming performances, they must get out of their slumps quickly. This responsibility falls on you and your dancers.

Knowledge and documentation on the subject within dance is conspicuously lacking. But the following should provide you with a clear understanding of slumps, what causes them, and how you can help your dancers get out of them.

Center Stage:
Identifying a Slump

As instructor, ask the following questions:

- What is the average level of performance?
- What are the typical highs and lows during the performance season?
- Are recent performances unusually low?
- Are there obvious causes of the decline in performance?

WHAT IS A SLUMP?

The term slump is used to describe a variety of performance-related problems. A slump is defined as an unexplained decline in a dancer's performance that extends longer than would be expected from normal variation in performance. This definition provides three criteria for identifying a slump, making it possible to recognize whether a drop in performance should be considered a slump.

Average Performance Comparison

First, consider what the dancer's typical performance level is and if the current level differs significantly. Because dancers' perceptions of their performance often differ from the reality, a dancer may think his or her performance is markedly below normal when only a slight difference may be evident. As a result, it is important for you to judge whether the dancer is, in fact, performing well below expected.

Variation in Performance

Next, determine the usual ups-and-downs in performance by looking at several dance-related factors, including number of performance mistakes and degree of virtuosity and artistry. Keeping track of this information will show past declines in performance and the typical period of time associated with these decreases. The current level of performance can then be compared to these expected variations to determine whether the decline is greater than normal variations during the season.

Cause of Decline

Once you have decided that the current level of performance is significantly below normal, conduct a cursory survey of causes. If the cause is obvious, then it can be dealt with, and the drop in performance reversed. However, if no clear reason for the decrease can be found, then it may be due to a slump.

FINDING THE CAUSES OF SLUMPS

The first step in alleviating a slump involves finding its cause. This stage is crucial because resolving slumps depends on finding their cause(s).

The causes of slumps can be physical, technical, equipment-related, and psychological. Each of these groups contains specific areas that can decrease performance and lead to a slump.

Physical

Perhaps the most frequent cause of slumps involves some physical problem. Because there are so many potential problem areas this cause is the most difficult to identify. The most common physical difficulties include fatigue due to overtraining or overperforming. Associated with this condition is the onset of illness caused by fatigue. Injuries are another significant cause of slumps. An unfortunate part of being a dancer often involves performing despite so-called minor injuries. Other less conspicuous physical problems include nutritional deficiencies that prevent the body from performing optimally, and sensory deficits, such as a decline in eyesight or hearing.

Technical

Declines in performance leading to slumps can be the result of some technical change. Technique is an extremely precise interplay of a variety of motor programs. Technique not only influences the actual execution of a skill but also the timing of its execution. If something is altered in one area, it can interfere with the whole performance, and until this change is identified, the performance decline will persist.

Equipment-Related

Slumps can also be caused by issues relating to equipment. In particular, the type of equipment dancers choose can affect performance. As dancers evolve to higher levels of performance, they develop a precise balance between their equipment, technique, and physical processes associated with timing and feel. As a result, a change in the characteristics of a dancer's equipment can have a profound effect on performance. For example, changing point shoes can significantly influence the precise equilibrium of optimal perform-ance.

Psychological

A variety of psychological factors, including performance-related problems and difficulties that occur away from the studio or stage, can inhibit perform-ance and may often prolong a slump. One significant psychological cause involves performer's misperceptions. Dancers may exaggerate the severity of a poor performance, when it might only be a temporary and expected fluctuation. Dancers may also inappropriately perceive their performance was poor when, from an objective perspective, it was good.

In addition, judgments that dancers make about their performances can influence slumps. Statements like, "I'm just not good enough" or "I didn't try hard enough" can cause negative perceptions about performance, which in turn may lead to a slump. Other performance-related factors that may cause slumps include a loss of self-confidence, inability to handle perform-ance pressure, and distractions while performing.

Events away from the studio and stage can also contribute to slumps. Family problems, social life, and finances can adversely affect dancers during performance and lead to daily difficulties, general life stress, and even serious pathologies.

Multiple Causes

One common mistake in determining the cause of slumps is accepting the most obvious cause as the primary cause. For example, it is often thought that slumps are primarily psychological in nature, because dancers in slumps exhibit a significant loss of self-confidence and concentration. Consequently, little attention is given to other potential problem areas. However, these psychological reactions are usually symptomatic of a more basic problem associated with performance. Therefore, slumps must be examined for their primary, secondary, and even more remote causes, and each must be ad-dressed systematically.

What makes this process so difficult is that there is no predictable sequence of causation. Various possible causes can affect performance in any order and in many ways. Start the identification process by conducting a compre-hensive examination of your dancers to discover the primary cause of the slump. Look closely at your dancers' physical, technical, equipment-related, and psychological conditions for potential causes.

The goal is to isolate every cause. Yet, this is not always possible. Invariably, there will be situations, particularly early in the slump, where a significant contributor remains a mystery. The best approach is to address the causes that are evident and, in time, the mystery cause will reveal itself or its influence will diminish. To better illustrate multiple causes of slumps, consider these actual case examples and their initial causes.

Physical.   Sean, a professional dancer, was performing poorly, lacking concentration and artistry. He had lost confidence in his performance ability, exhibited unusually high anxiety, and was easily distracted. The dancer felt physically healthy, but nevertheless underwent a complete physical exam. Though the physician said he was in excellent health, hearing tests indicated the dancer had experienced a hearing loss which affected his balance, his cues, and his timing with other dancers. Initially, the slump was viewed as caused by psychological problems. Only through careful scrutiny did the true physiological cause become evident. Losing auditory acuity was the primary cause of Sean's drop in performance, which in turn, hurt his ability to perform well, resulting in decreased self-confidence, increased anxiety when performing, and an inability to concentrate.

Psychological.   A jazz dancer, Margaret, had a history of tendonitis that limited her performance. Though the problem was never considered serious by her doctor, the cause of the injury could not be pinpointed, and the usual prognosis was rest and physical therapy. After a few days of rest, the tendonitis seemed to heal and the dancer returned to the studio. Upon investigation, a pattern became evident where the tendonitis problem developed most often just prior to a major performance. Her peers and teachers also noticed changes in her demeanor. For example, she exhibited greater emotional reactivity and negativity. The dancer revealed that she felt considerable pressure to perform well and became very anxious during this time. This anxiety produced subtle changes in her technique, which in turn, resulted in inflammation of the tendon. Based on this analysis, it was concluded that the injury was a by-product of a more pervasive psychological issue. Though the physical ailment appeared to be the primary cause, it was actually a secondary cause that resulted from a technical problem, which was caused by a negative psychological response.

Equipment-related.   Following a very successful first half of the season, a young ballet dancer, Carrie, exhibited a significant drop in performance during the second half of the season. She had lost her self-confidence and was dancing tentatively and without enthusiasm. After considerable discussion with the dancer, it became clear to Carrie's teachers that though the psychological issues were hurting her, they did not seem significant enough to explain her poor dancing. They further examined the occurrences leading up to the slump and concluded that the problem might be her point shoes. The dancer had changed her point shoes and this affected her dancing. This event was overlooked because the new shoes were comfortable. But, the different feel of the new point shoes had subtly affected Carrie's dancing. Again, a slump that appeared to be caused by one issue, in this case psychological, turned out to be initiated by another, here an equipment problem.

PREVENTING SLUMPS

The best way to deal with a problem is to prevent it. You can help your dancers prevent, or at least reduce greatly, the likelihood of slumps by taking some active steps.

Perhaps the most common cause of slumps is physical wear-and-tear. Grueling rehearsals, regular performances, and travel exact a significant toll on your dancers in terms of fatigue, illness, and injury. As a result, pay close attention to your dancers' physical condition to prevent slumps. Following a rigorous off-season physical training program and a performance-season physical maintenance program will help dancers minimize slumps due to physical breakdown. The better shape dancers are in, the more they will be able to resist the physical stresses of the performance season.

The most neglected aspect of dance training and a major part of slump prevention is rest. During the performance season, dancers rarely get the opportunity to unwind and allow their bodies to rebuild. Also, highly motivated dancers resist taking days off believing that they will get out of shape and lose their virtuosity.

Make rest a regular part of the performance season. Schedule mandatory days off, ideally at least one day per week. Increase the quality and decrease the quantity of class and rehearsal time. And plan a responsible performance schedule that allows dancers to recover from performance series. A mid-season break of three to six days should also be incorporated into the performance season. Finally, a valuable lesson to teach your dancers is to "listen" to their bodies. Young dancers think they are invincible and, consequently, do not believe that they need rest or time off. By educating them about the warning signs of slumps, such as early indications of fatigue, illness, and injury, they can take preventive steps. Although rest may entail some time away from the studio, it will enable them to perform their best through the end of the season.

Also, as suggested throughout this text, dancers should consistently engage in an organized PPEP. Maintaining their mental health, as they do their physical health, will reduce the likelihood that a slump will start due to psychological causes. Maintaining proper care of their equipment, such as toe shoes, will make slumps caused by equipment breakdown less likely. Finally, paying attention to proper technique, particularly late in the season when your dancers begin to wear down, will decrease the probability of slumps due to technical reasons.

Center Stage:
Preventing Slumps

Have your dancers

- maintain good physical condition during the performance season,
- get plenty of rest,
- take regular days off,
- listen to their body, and
- maintain proper care of equipment.

As instructor, strive to

- increase quality, decrease quantity of training;
- plan a responsible performance schedule; and
- be sensitive to subtle changes in technique, particularly late in the performance season.

SLUMPBUSTING PLAN

Identifying the primary causes of slumps is a crucial step toward alleviating them, but only the first step. Because secondary and more remote causes can, in a sense, assume a life of their own, it is necessary to directly address each cause of the slump in a structured way. Unless each cause is treated in sequence, a link in the slump chain may be overlooked and the slump will continue. Have your dancers complete the Causes of Performance Slump worksheet to determine all the factors that may be causing their slump.

Many believe that dancers can easily move out of their slumps. To the contrary, one aspect of slumps is that they are extended, and just as it takes time to get into them, it takes time to get out of them. For the alleviation process to be most effective, you and your dancers must accept this notion

Causes of Performance Slump

Directions: In the space below, indicate what you believe are the specific causes of your dance performance slump.

Physical (injury, fatigue, illness)

Technical (poor position, execution)

Equipment (shoes, costume)

Psychological (confidence, intensity, concentration)

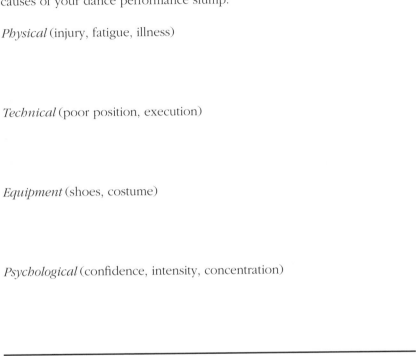

and be willing to put in the time and effort necessary for dancers to return to form.

This is an important aspect of the "slumpbusting plan." To illustrate how such a plan can be implemented, consider again the example of Sean, whose hearing acuity had decreased. This physical problem led to a technical change in his performance, and to psychological problems: loss of self-confidence, excessive anxiety, and inability to concentrate, which as secondary causes reinforced the strength of his slump.

Time-Out

An important first step in slumpbusting is the use of time-out. In other words, dancers should take a brief period of time off away from training and performance, and experience a different environment with different people, if possible. Because a critical component of a slump is the strong negative emotional atmosphere it creates within the dancer, being away from the pressures of the studio gives dancers,an emotional vacation. The time-out allows them to gain some perspective on the slump and turn the negative view of past performances into a positive attitude about future rehearsals and performances.

Slumps are as draining physically as they are mentally, so the time-out enables dancers to rest, relax, and "recharge their batteries." It gives them the opportunity to catch up on their rest, overcome lingering illnesses, and rehabilitate nagging injuries. By being away from the studio for a brief time, dancers can gain an objective perspective on their performances. They can then use this time and information to develop a plan to relieve the slump in the shortest possible time.

The duration of the time-out period should be proportional to the severity of the slump. In general, time-outs of 2 to 5 days are most helpful, though even a few hours away from the studio can be effective. In addition, the time-out will be most effective when the dancers have a significant change of scenery and people. In other words, they should have physical, psychological, and emotional distance from the conditions that caused the slump. The greater the change in setting, the better the results.

Sean took five days away from the studio and visited friends in Florida. While there, he rested a lot, had fun, and kept his mind off dance for the first few days. By the end of the third day, he started feeling better physically, had a much more relaxed and positive attitude, and began to miss dance. On the fourth day, he sat down and laid out his slumpbusting plan. By the fifth day, he couldn't wait to get back to the studio to start dancing again.

Specify Goals

Once the causes of the slump are clearly understood, your dancers need to specify a series of goals to deal with those causes and alleviate the slump. Have them complete the following Slumpbusting Goal-Setting Program worksheet.

Return-to-form goals.   This goal clarifies the ultimate objective of the program. Specifically, the return-to-form goal stipulates the level of performance to which dancers wish to return. It may be the usual level at which they performed prior to the slump, or it may be different because of new information that emerged since the slump. As with all subsequent goals that will be discussed, this one should be specific, measurable, and realistic.

Sean specified this goal as returning to his previous level of performance in two roles he would be dancing in the coming month. Using videotapes comparing prior rehearsal of the roles with his current rehearsals, the dance mistress, the choreographer, and Sean himself would measure and evaluate

Slumpbusting Goal-Setting Program

Directions:　In the space below, indicate your specific goals for overcoming your slump.

Return-to-form (where you want to be)

1.

2.

3.

4.

Causal (what you need to do to relieve every cause)

1.

2.

3.

4.

Daily training (what you need to do every day)

1.

2.

3.

4.

Daily performance (how you want to perform)

1.

2.

3.

4.

his improvement. Furthermore, he set a 3-week time frame for achieving this goal.

Causal goals. This goal addresses what will be done, in terms of level of performance, to alleviate a particular cause of the slump. For example, if the slump is caused by a physical problem, then the causal goal might involve a measurable level of strength or flexibility that will be worked toward. If the slump is due to technical or psychological issues, then causal goals will be directed toward resolving those areas. Most importantly, there should be a causal goal for every cause, whether it is primary, secondary, or more remote.

Since there were three causes for Sean's slump, each was assigned a causal goal. The goal for alleviating the physical cause, the auditory impairment, was reached with a brief period of medication and auditory therapy. This enabled the dancer to focus on the other causal goals. The dancer's goal to correct his technical faults was to reestablish his previous level of technical accuracy and regain his feeling of artistry on the stage. His psychological goals included rebuilding his self-confidence, relaxing more while performing, and concentrating better on task-relevant cues.

Daily training goals. Once the causal goals have been defined, dancers should specify daily goals to reach their causal goals. These goals detail what training or rehearsing dancers must do each day in order to ameliorate the causes and resolve their slumps. First, dancers must determine the best way to deal with the slump. When dealing with a technical problem, for instance, you and your dancers must decide the best means to correct the technical flaw. Similarly, for a physical difficulty, dancers may enlist the aid of a sports medicine practitioner in choosing the best rehabilitative techniques. In addition, daily goals should bring dancers toward their causal and return-to-form goals in a progressive, constructive manner.

Sean achieved his daily technical goals with two private classes per week with the dance mistress reviewing videotapes of his sessions and paying particular attention to space and timing. From there he moved daily toward greater artistry in performance. He did not move up to the next level of daily goals until he was able to accomplish his current goal consistently. A similar plan was implemented for his daily psychological goals. Sean accomplished these through three sessions per week of progressive relaxation and dance imagery training, and incorporating thought-stopping and positive self-reinforcement into class and rehearsal. Sean used an analogous progression for his imagery sessions and employed a sequence of appropriate concentration cues to facilitate focusing on and accomplishing the daily training goals.

Daily performance goals. Often dancers are unable to take time off from their performance schedules to resolve their slumps. They must continue performing regularly while trying to address the causes of the slump. This can be difficult and sometimes counterproductive because, while working to remedy the slump, dancers may still be performing below expectations. This may prolong a negative orientation toward their performance, interfering with the long-term resolution of the slump.

It is essential to establish daily performance goals to provide dancers with a level of performance to work toward, which although below their desired level, would be above their current slump-induced level. These daily performance goals provide realistic levels toward which to strive, making performances rewarding and reinforcing rather than discouraging. In addition, these goals produce a positive orientation that will facilitate the dancers' climb out of a slump.

After taking time-out in Florida, Sean's performance schedule picked up and he no longer had the luxury of not dancing while working his way out of the slump. However, by setting specific, progressive goals for each performance, his dancing became a positive, contributing component of the slumpbusting plan. Like his daily training goals, these goals focused on rebuilding his dancing technically, artistically, and psychologically. More importantly, they enabled him to rehearse the skills and attitudes he had worked on, reinforcing the positive results and feelings he had developed. Consequently, his performance facilitated, rather than inhibited, his return-to-form, and he demonstrated improved dancing in each performance. Within the three week goal time frame, he achieved all of his daily performance, daily training, and causal goals, which resulted in accomplishing his return-to-form goal and overcoming the slump.

Emotional Counseling

As discussed, a significant contributor to slumps is the negative emotional chain that develops as the slump worsens. To break this chain quickly, incorporate both individual and group counseling into the slumpbusting plan. Individual counseling with a professional who understands dance allows dancers to express their thoughts and feelings about the events they are experiencing to an impartial, objective observer. The counselor can then provide effective coping skills dancers can use to better deal with their concerns and anxiety.

The company of which Sean was a member had a professional counselor on staff. He met with the counselor twice a week during the slumpbusting period. In the sessions, he expressed his concerns about how the slump would affect his position within the company and his goal of moving up to a major metropolitan company. The counselor, in turn, provided an objective perspective on what he was experiencing and helped him realistically look at the consequences of the slump.

Group counseling allows dancers to share their experiences about slumps. These sessions serve several valuable purposes. They provide a meaningful social support system within which dancers can work to mitigate their slumps. This support alleviates the extreme sense of isolation that often accompanies slumps. It also furnishes a strong, centralized source of encouragement, and moral and mutual support. In group sessions dancers share their concerns about slumps and learn that the worries and misgivings they feel are not unique, but are in fact, natural and expected. Furthermore, dancers can share and compare techniques they have found useful in relieving slumps, increasing their own sense of responsibility and control over slumps.

Sean took part in a weekly group session and explained what he had been going through lately. Several seasoned dancers indicated that they went through slumps about twice a year. They also provided him with several techniques he could use to overcome the slump.

 Center Stage:
Slumpbusting Plan

Have your dancers do the following:

- Identify all possible causes of slumps: physical, technical, equipment-related, and psychological.
- Use the PPEP techniques.
- Take time-out: Get away from the performance environment.
- Set goals to get out of a slump: return-to-form, causal, daily training, daily performance.
- Obtain individual and group counseling.

STRESS AND BURNOUT

Slumps are not only significant because they hurt dance performance; they may also lead to stress and burnout. *Stress* is a negative psychological, emotional, or physical reaction to pressure. *Burnout* is characterized as an accumulation of stress that results in a condition of physical, psychological, and emotional exhaustion. Stress and burnout are most common among highly dedicated dancers. Stress and burnout also result from an inability to cope with persistent stressors or the perception that the demands of a situation exceed one's ability to overcome them. Considering these two factors, it is easy to see that dancers are prime candidates for stress and burnout.

To illustrate how stress and burnout may affect your dancers, consider Emily, a gifted 16-year-old ballet dancer in a small, though well-respected, dance school. Emily comes from a family in which both parents are successful professionals. Her mother danced professionally for many years and Emily's older sister, Lauren, is currently with the city's professional company. She is a straight A student who spends all of her time either studying or dancing. She has few friends and little social life. Emily sets very high standards for herself and can become despondent when these objectives are not met.

In addition to the psychological characteristics of stress and burnout, environmental and social factors may also contribute. Environmental contributors include long performance seasons, monotonous training routines, overly rigid studio rules, and training overload. Social factors include lack of reinforcement from instructors, parents, and peers; conflict within a dance school or company; and maltreatment and pressure from instructors and parents.

Emily's school recently hired a former Bolshoi dancer, Ms. Yereva, who believes that what worked for her will work for her young American students. Her classes are very regimented and her dancers are expected to follow, without deviation, her rigorous training program. Both Ms. Yereva and Emily's parents recognize that she has talent, so they are constantly placing greater demands on her, but do not provide much encouragement or positive feedback.

The performing arts environment amplifies the stress often faced in other fields. Dancers are placed in a dramatically visible setting in which they are "under the microscope." This is particularly true for principal dancers. Additionally, in the close confines of a dance company or school, personality differences and conflicts are magnified. Tremendous physical and emotional strain is also incurred during long hours of classes and rehearsals.

> I put pressure on me. Nobody does it to you but you. I did it because of how I interpreted what was written in the newspaper about me. . . . I was trying to match the image that was written about me. And I got my head way out of proportion instead of just enjoying and loving to dance. (Judith Jamison in Lyle, 1977, p. 101)

Warning Signs of Stress and Burnout

Become aware of any indication of stress and burnout among your dancers. Warning signs are divided into four categories: physical, emotional, cognitive, and performance (see Table 6.1).

Physical. Physical warning signs of stress and burnout are the easiest to spot. Frequent illness is a strong indicator of potential problems. In general,

Table 6.1　Warning Signs of Burnout

Category	Sign
Physical	Frequent illness
	Frequent injuries
	Frequent physical complaints (headaches, stomach aches)
	Sleeping problems
Emotional	Anger
	Depression
	Moodiness
Cognitive	Excessively negative or self-critical
	Low self-confidence
	Unrealistic expectations
	Noncommunicative
	Social withdrawal
Performance	Nervous, tight performances
	Trying too hard
	Worse dancing in performance than in class or rehearsal
	Lack of enjoyment in training and performance
	Low motivation
	Loss of interest and enthusiasm in dance and other areas
	"Give-up" syndrome
	Drop in school performance

dancers are capable of fighting off most types of illness under normal conditions. However, when dancers are under significant stress, they are more prone to illness. Constant injuries also may indicate high stress and impending burnout. Anxiety, concentration problems, and overall fatigue make dancers more susceptible to injury. Additionally, recurrent sleeping problems, such as insomnia or nightmares, or eating difficulties, like unusual weight gain or loss, may indicate stress and potential burnout.

Recently, Emily had a number of minor, but recurring injuries that interfered with her training. Also, she had nightmares about falling off the stage during a performance right in front of her parents, causing everyone to laugh at her and humiliate her parents.

Emotional.　Out-of-character displays of emotionality may suggest unhealthy stress in your dancers. Moodiness, irritability, excessive sensitivity to criticism, depression, and inappropriate emotions may all indicate a negative stress reaction. Due to the nature of dance, you should expect some emotional swings in your dancers. However, if these emotional changes persist, you may assume that they indicate a problem.

Emily had been depressed lately, but when asked by her parents what was wrong, she only said to them that she was tired and focusing on her schoolwork and her dance. She also felt very angry but was afraid to express it to anyone.

Cognitive.   The way that your dancers think and talk about themselves can warn of stress and burnout. Excessive negativity and other indications of lowered self-confidence may signal a problem. Unusually high expectations prior to a performance, and unrealistic and harsh evaluations after a performance may also indicate stress.

Emily was extremely critical of her dancing in class and rehearsal. Even when Ms. Yereva and other students praised her performances, she brushed them off and found things she was doing wrong.

Performance.   An obvious indication of stress in your dancers is changes in their class, rehearsal, and performance dancing. In the studio, reduced motivation, lack of enjoyment, loss of enthusiasm and interest in dance and other areas of their lives, and a tendency to give up in the face of minimal difficulties should tell you that something is wrong. During performances, dancers who are uncharacteristically nervous, dance worse in performances than in class or rehearsals, and are unusually distracted may be under excessive stress and could be potential candidates for burnout.

Emily's dancing was deteriorating steadily. She made mistakes performing even easy movements. She no longer seemed to enjoy going to class, and at a recent performance in which she was the principal dancer, Emily was so nervous, her understudy had to dance the role.

Center Stage:
Preventing and Treating Stress and Burnout

As instructor, strive to

- be sensitive to your dancers' physical and emotional condition,
- not overtrain your dancers,
- make training fun,
- schedule regular days off,
- provide constant encouragement and positive reinforcement,
- allow your dancers to be involved in decision making,
- open lines of communication with parents and other significant people, and
- seek out professional help when needed.

Treating Stress and Burnout

> I'm very excited about dance and love it with a deep passion. I also struggle, tire and become discouraged. But what has always revived me . . . has been the rebirth of energy each time the creative process is awakened and artistic activity begins to unfold even in some infinitesimal measure. (Ann Halprin in Ellfeldt, 1976, p. 208)

Once the warning signs of stress and burnout have been detected, take active steps to combat the symptoms and the causes. At the insistence of an instructor who had befriended Emily, and with whom Emily had shared her feelings, the school's counselor arranged a meeting with Emily's parents. After discussing the changes in Emily's behavior in the studio and at home, it became clear that she was suffering and needed help. The counselor described the further negative effects that could ensue and explained the role that Ms. Yereva and her parents had in contributing to Emily's condition. With the cooperation of Ms. Yereva and Emily's parents, the counselor recommended some changes that would, hopefully, help Emily regain her happiness and her former level of dance performance.

A basic principle to follow for both the prevention and treatment of stress and burnout is that success is not found in the performance, but in the striving for the performance. In other words, emphasis should be placed on the effort put into the preparation and process of the performance, rather than its outcome. When dancers are asked what they remember most about a great performance, they usually do not describe the accolades or the rave reviews. They discuss the hard work put into the performance and the feeling of dancing well. Dancers cannot always control their outcomes, for example, whether they get a role, but they can control how hard they try.

With the assistance of the counselor, Ms. Yereva and Emily's parents increased the amount of encouragement and positive reinforcement they gave her and began rewarding her efforts rather than her performances.

Practical ways to prevent and reduce stress and burnout include being sensitive to your dancers, physically and emotionally. Be careful not to overtrain them. If you see indications of fatigue, give them time away from the studio to rest and to enable them to recognize how much they love and miss dance. When they return, ease off on the quantity and intensity of their training. Training should be fun and not a chore. If you see less enthusiasm and enjoyment, add variety to training and emphasize pleasure. Also involve your dancers in some of the decision making in class. For example, give them choices about what exercises will be included in class. Always be positive and constructive rather than negative and critical.

Ms. Yereva instructed Emily to take a week off to rest her injuries. During this time, Emily's parents spent more time with her and gave her the opportunity to do some fun things for which she usually had little time. Upon returning to the studio, Ms. Yereva required that she only attend class three rather than five times a week for the next month. Emily also worked more with the instructor who had befriended her and was allowed to choose some of the exercises that she liked most.

Taking these steps will not always relieve your dancers of their stress. Often, stress builds up from a variety of areas within and outside the studio. Establish open lines of communication with parents or other involved individuals so that each of you can fully understand what dancers are experiencing, and then work together to deal with the problems that emerge. Finally, you should seek out an appropriately trained professional whenever there is serious concern about the physical, mental, and emotional well-being of your dancers.

Because of the severity of Emily's condition, the school's counselor was brought in. This resulted in immediate, direct, and constructive action to help Emily. It also enlightened Ms. Yereva and Emily's parents about how best to assist Emily, and other dancers, in reaching their full potential as dancers and ensuring that their dance experience is one that enhances their personal and social development.

ENCORE

Slumps, extreme drops in dance performance, are a natural part of being a dancer. A slump is an unexplained decline in performance that extends longer than would be expected from a dancer's normal ups and downs.

Use three criteria to identify a slump: (a) whether a dancer's typical performance level is well above the current level, (b) whether that difference is more than would be expected due to the usual ups and downs of dance performance, and (c) whether there is a clear reason for the decline in performance.

The four primary causes of slumps include: physical, technical, equipment-related, and psychological. Slumps often have more than one cause, so they must be examined for their primary, secondary, and more remote causes. The goal in this process is to identify and address every cause.

Slumps can be prevented by encouraging your dancer to: participate in a performance season physical maintenance program, "listen" to their bodies, make rest a regular part of their training, engage in an organized PPEP, maintain their equipment in top condition, and pay attention to their technique throughout the performance season.

It takes time to get into slumps. You and your dancers must realize that it will take time and effort to get out of them. To alleviate a slump, develop an organized slumpbusting plan. A slumpbusting plan must include four goals: return-to-form, causal, daily training, and daily performance.

Time-out, getting away from the dance setting for two to five days, helps overcome slumps by: breaking the negative emotional chain, allowing dancers to rest and "recharge their batteries," and giving them time to develop an organized plan of action to resolve the slump.

Individual and group counseling can help dancers deal with the emotional aspects of a slump by allowing them to express their worries and concerns, and to receive social support and perspective from others.

Extended slumps may lead to stress and burnout in dancers. Stress is a negative psychological, emotional, or physical reaction to pressure. Burnout is characterized as an accumulation of stress that results in a condition of physical, psychological, and emotional exhaustion. Stress and burnout are most common among highly dedicated dancers.

Other factors that contribute to stress and burnout include long performance seasons, monotonous training, training overload, boredom, lack of reinforcement, conflict within the studio, and pressure from instructors and parents.

Warning signs of stress and burnout may be physical (fatigue, illness, and injury), emotional (moodiness and depression), cognitive (negative self-talk and harsh performance evaluations), or performance (lack of enthusiasm and interest in class and dancing worse during performances than rehearsals).

Prevent and treat stress and burnout by emphasizing effort rather than outcome of performances, not overtraining, adding variety and fun to classes, establishing lines of communication with parents or other involved individuals, and seeking out professional help if the well-being of the dancer is in question.

7

Psychology of Dance Injury Rehabilitation

Is there life after a serious injury? There can be, if the body recovers sufficiently. But full recovery means more than being able to bend and straighten a knee or land full force on the delicate bones of a weakened foot. Indeed, the process of regaining one's psychological confidence after recovery from a serious injury is extraordinarily difficult. And the dancer alone does not determine his fate: His boss, the artistic director, must regain confidence as well. (Gere, 1992, pp. 33-34)

Dress Rehearsal:
Enhancing Injury Rehabilitation

Carl is a 25-year-old modern dancer in a touring company. Near the end of their recent tour, he tore his ligaments in his left ankle and received surgery to repair the damage. Carl, feeling pressure to return for the next tour in four months, became discouraged at what he perceived to be too slow a rehabilitation. Carl also became anxious at the prospect of his career ending. As a result, he pushed too hard in his physical therapy and tried to return to the stage too soon.

1. What psychological issues need to be addressed for him to rehabilitate fully?
2. What techniques would you put into a rehabilitation program to assist Carl in making a full psychological and physical recovery?

Due to the rigorous training programs that are an integral part of every dancers' commitment to dance, injuries are a pervasive part of a career in dance. Virtually all dancers will experience an injury that will keep them out of the studio and off the stage for an extended period at some time in their careers. "Every dancer's worst nightmare: a sudden injury leading to a series of related injuries . . ." (Gere, 1992, p. 32).

Fortunately, surgical and rehabilitative technology has developed to such an extent that full physical recovery from dance injuries can often be expected. Unfortunately, despite the potential for full physical recovery, dancers often do not return to their preinjury level of performance, even when all measurable aspects of the injured area indicate full recovery of strength, flexibility, and stability. This may be due to psychological barriers that developed from the injury and the lack of rehabilitation of psychological factors that influence performance. Antoinette Sibley said, "The difficulty was more mental every time, coming back from an injury, more the mental thing of being pushed down and trying to come up again" (Newman, 1982, p. 264).

PSYCHOLOGICAL FACTORS IN INJURY REHABILITATION

As discussed, motivation, self-confidence, anxiety (intensity), and concentration are very important to dance performance. These psychological factors also have a significant impact on injury rehabilitation. To illustrate the importance and value of the psychological rehabilitation of physical injury, consider Alan, a 30-year-old professional jazz dancer, who tore the anterior cruciate ligament of his right knee during rehearsals for a Broadway show.

Self-Confidence

As discussed in chapter 2, self-confidence is important because it affects all other psychological factors related to dance performance and affects performance directly. The same holds true for injury rehabilitation. Helgi Tomasson, artistic director of the San Francisco Ballet, said of recovering from injury: "When injuries happen to dancers, sometimes there is a change that takes place. There is less assurance, less confidence. Sometimes . . . the freedom or the spirit is affected. And I'm not saying that can't be brought back. I've seen that happen" (Gere, 1992, p. 36). Self-confidence is necessary at three levels in the rehabilitation process. First, injured dancers must have confidence in their ability to adhere to and successfully complete the long and sometimes painful physical rehabilitation program. If dancers do not believe that they can have a full physical recovery, even with an extensive rehabilitation program, they will not work hard.

Second, injured dancers must have confidence in the effectiveness of the rehabilitation program. Believing in the success of the program is as important as believing in their ability to complete the program. "Of course the unknown bothered me. You can think about the ifs and maybes, and it can drive you crazy, or give you strength. So I concentrated on getting cured" (Gary Chryst on his rehabilitation, in Flatow, 1982, p. 18).

Third, dancers must believe that if they complete the rehabilitation program they will again be able to perform at their previous level. If they do not believe this they will have little motivation to work hard on the rehabilitation program.

Alan, the professional jazz dancer, at 30 years of age was relatively old for a dancer, and he knew, even without the injury, he only had a few years left to dance at his current high level. After the injury, he began to doubt whether he would ever dance again, even though his surgeon and physical therapist expressed great confidence in his ability to rehabilitate fully. He became quite despondent and pessimistic about his chances of recovery.

Motivation

Due to the length and intensity of the rehabilitation process, dancers must establish and maintain a high level of motivation. This is often difficult because of lack of self-confidence and confidence in the rehabilitation program, anxiety about the recovery, and problems concentrating, all of which may reduce motivation, inhibiting full recovery.

In the initial stages of his rehabilitation, Alan missed several physical therapy sessions, and when he did come, he put less than full effort into them. After only three weeks, he was well behind the expected progress. He often came to the clinic with little energy or motivation, and had to be prodded by the physical therapist just to complete the exercises. He was also putting on weight and getting out of shape.

Anxiety

Experiencing serious injury and going through a lengthy recovery is anxiety-provoking in many ways. The most obvious cause is the pain associated with the injury. During a rehabilitation program, constant pain is present from the injury itself and the therapeutic exercises. Pain places tremendous stress on the body and can inhibit the healing process. Anxiety also occurs when injured dancers worry about the success of the program. This issue relates back to their confidence in the rehabilitation program and their ability to successfully complete it.

> Mentally, there was an incredible amount of anguish and fear. The sheer action of getting up on that foot and turning around twice—sometimes I would just have to go in a corner because I would be choked up and close to tears. It's frustration. But you have to be intelligent about it, because if you pull back in fear from anything in dance, you're going to hurt yourself. (Gary Chryst in Flatow, 1982, p. 40)

Injury and recovery also produce anxiety by taking away aspects of dancers' lives that are rewarding and supportive: the psychological and emotional rewards of dance; the physical benefits of class, rehearsal, and performance; and the camaraderie and friendships with other dancers. So not only do injured dancers have to endure the rehabilitation process, they must do it in an environment that is no longer reinforcing.

Of particular concern is the loss of social support during rehabilitation. Healthy dancers have a tendency to avoid injured dancers, superstitiously believing that the injury will be contagious. Leaving an injured dancer alone and isolated can be detrimental to the recovery process because evidence suggests that social support facilitates rehabilitation. Though it is not fully clear why this occurs, support from others may increase self-confidence and motivation, and reduce anxiety. Also, well-supported individuals appear to have better functioning immune systems.

Unfortunately, anxiety does not stop when the rehabilitation program is nearly completed and full recovery seems imminent. Dancers have new concerns when they return to the studio and the stage. Foremost are doubts about their ability to return to preinjury form. Again, this relates to self-confidence. Also, during postinjury training and performance, there may be a fear of reinjury. This worry diminishes dancers' confidence in their ability to perform and distracts concentration from performance focus, which increases the risk of injury.

Anxiety also has a direct physical debilitating effect. For example, anxiety restricts breathing, impairing the intake of oxygen. With less oxygen, healing takes longer. Anxiety causes extreme muscle tension, which increases pain and reduces blood flow to the injured area. Additionally, stress slows healing by decreasing the efficiency of the immune system.

Because of his lack of confidence in the recovery process, Alan experienced considerable anxiety and worry. He often felt tense, especially when he went to the clinic for rehabilitation therapy. This anxiety caused an unusual amount of pain, which slowed his progress. Alan also felt isolated and unsupported because he couldn't get to the studio. He missed his friends and the camaraderie of preparing for a Broadway show, and would spend most days moping around his apartment.

Concentration

Concentration affects the quality of rehabilitation. Dancers tend to focus on negative aspects of injury rather than on positive aspects of the rehabilitation process. When this occurs, self-confidence and motivation are negatively affected, resulting in reduced effort. Also, without proper focus, dancers have difficulty maintaining a high level of intensity during rehabilitation, which slows the recovery process.

Concentration is also important during post-recovery training and performance. Again, thinking about the injured area rather than the performance increases the likelihood of reinjury. It also lowers self-confidence and increases anxiety, further raising the potential for reinjury.

Alan's early rehabilitation was not going well. He was dwelling on the negative consequences of the injury rather than on what he had to do to recover fully. During rehabilitation at the clinic, he would talk about how bad his situation was instead of putting focus and intensity into his exercises.

PSYCHOLOGICAL REHABILITATION PROGRAM (PREP)

A serious injury produces both physical and psychological challenges. Well-organized physical rehabilitation is necessary for full injury recovery. Similarly, to ensure a complete return to a preinjury level of performance, a structured *psychological rehabilitation program (PReP)* should be a part of the recovery process. This program would be similar to a PPEP and could follow the procedure discussed in chapter 8. Five primary strategies should comprise a PReP: (a) goal setting, (b) relaxation training, (c) dance imagery, (d) a variety of general PPEP techniques, and (e) social support. The purpose of these techniques is to optimize the four psychological areas (self-confidence, motivation, anxiety, and concentration) that influence the rehabilitation process, increasing the quality and decreasing the length of the recovery process.

> "There are three steps you have to complete to become a professional dancer: learn to dance, learn to perform, and learn how to cope with injuries" (Gere, 1992, p. 34).

After four weeks of rehabilitation, the prospects of a complete recovery for Alan did not look good. He was capable of full recovery, but decreased confidence, low motivation, increased anxiety, and negative focus limited his progress. After attending a workshop on the psychological aspects of injury rehabilitation, the studio's dance mistress and physical therapist helped Alan organize a PReP (see Table 7.1).

Goal Setting

To organize an effective PReP, dancers should set a variety of goals to provide direction and focus. Goal setting benefits injured dancers several ways. It increases commitment and motivation to the rehabilitation program. It gives injured dancers a feeling of control over their injury, which may in-

Table 7.1   Alan's Psychological Rehabilitation Program

Rehabilitation area	Technique
Self-confidence	Dancer's litany Thought-stopping
Motivation	Goal setting Rehabilitation partner
Anxiety	Breathing Progressive relaxation
Concentration	Key words
Social support	Group meetings Staying involved in dance
Overall rehabilitation and performance	Dance imagery: healing and performance

crease self-confidence and reduce anxiety. It also helps injured dancers focus on important parts of rehabilitation and divert attention from negative aspects of the injury. Dancers often want to rush through rehabilitation in order to return to the stage as quickly as possible, even at the expense of a complete recovery from the injury. "I've always said that slower is faster . . . trying to come back from an injury. . . . To succeed you must take deliberate steps with no shortcuts" (Edward Villella in Montee, 1992, p. 44). Goal setting provides those deliberate steps and ensures that dancers take the necessary time to fully recover from the injury before returning to the studio and stage. Four types of rehabilitation goals should be established: physical, psychological, maintenance/return-to-form, and performance.

Physical goals.   Specific goals for each aspect of the physical rehabilitation need to be set. These goals should include rehabilitation issues such as range of motion, strength, stamina, and flexibility. For each of these areas, there should be daily, weekly, and monthly goals set toward which the injured dancer will work. The dancer's rehabilitative professional, such as a physical therapist, should be consulted to ensure that these goals are appropriate.

Psychological goals.   Psychological recovery goals must also be set. These should be based on perceived barriers in the four psychological areas: self-confidence, motivation, anxiety, and concentration. Recognize and plan to deal with any obstacles that might inhibit the rehabilitation process. Particular techniques from previous chapters and ones that will be discussed shortly should be considered and included if appropriate.

Maintenance/return-to-form goals.   Goals should be set to minimize the deterioration of current physical, technical, and psychological abilities. Additionally, injured dancers should establish goals that will facilitate their return-to-form. Setting technical, physical, psychological, and performance goals to maintain and return-to-form will be beneficial. Dancers should identify what technical skills they will need to develop to maintain their progress and what technical skills they will need to reestablish after the injury. These skills can be worked on with dance imagery, live and video observation of other dancers, and limited physical practice of these skills within the constraints of the injury.

When dancers are healthy, they rarely have sufficient time to improve areas that are not directly related to the immediate performance. This down-time is a good time to identify physical weaknesses unrelated to the injury and work on them. This will result in an overall improvement of a dancer's physical conditioning upon returning to the studio. It will also give dancers a feeling that they are not only working to recover from an injury, but they are also training to improve their future dancing. For example, a male dancer recovering from a knee injury could spend time in the weight room strengthening his upper body to improve his lifts when he returns.

Injured dancers may also take this physical down-time to focus on and improve psychological and emotional areas that affect their performance. Talk to your dancers about their psychological strengths and weaknesses and assist them in identifying areas, such as self-confidence or intensity, that they could work on using PPEP techniques discussed in this book. This way, dancers can be even more psychologically prepared to perform well when they recover from their injury.

Performance goals.   The final goals that should be set relate to returning to the stage. Dancers who have recovered from an injury should not expect to immediately take on demanding roles. Rather, they should set a series of performance goals that progressively move them toward their desired level of performance.

Injured dancers must understand the necessity of developing a sound goal-setting program. Being committed to these goals and concentrating on these objectives will lead to a complete recovery and a successful return to the stage. For all of these goals, injured dancers should follow the goal guidelines and structure offered in chapter 1. Additional useful information may be adapted from chapter 6 on slumps, stress, and burnout.

The first task for Alan was to set a series of rehabilitation and performance goals. He established a program that included daily, weekly, and monthly rehabilitation improvement goals including consistent physical therapy attendance and developing range of motion, strength, and stamina of the repaired knee; for example, to increase quadriceps strength by 20%. He then set specific technical, physical, psychological, and performance goals for the time he would put in at the studio now and when he returned to regular classes and rehearsal.

 Center Stage:
Psychological Rehabilitation Program (PReP)

Have your dancers

- set rehabilitation goals: physical, psychological, maintenance/return-to-form, and performance;

- practice relaxation techniques;

- use dance imagery for injury rehabilitation (imagine injured area healing) and dance performance;

- use PPEP techniques to maintain self-confidence, stay motivated, reduce anxiety, and sustain concentration; and

- take part in a social support network.

Relaxation Training

An important technique to promote healing involves actively inducing relaxation. Greater anxiety is related to slower rehabilitation. As mentioned earlier, anxiety can result from the difficulty of the rehabilitation process and concerns about time away from the studio and stage. Anxiety may not manifest itself clearly enough for you or others to see and is not often distinctly felt by the injured dancer. Yet it may still have a dramatic impact on the rehabilitation process. As a result, you and your injured dancers should assume there is anxiety and take steps to relieve it.

Refer to chapter 3 for specific techniques that your injured dancers may use to relieve anxiety. The two most important exercises they should use are breathing and progressive relaxation. They should particularly apply the progressive relaxation to the injured area to relax the muscles around the injury, further promoting healing. Injured dancers should use the relaxation techniques during rehabilitation to reduce pain and encourage blood flow. They should also engage in relaxation immediately following rehabilitation, when muscles are tense and fatigued and pain is probably at a high level.

A primary goal for Alan was to reduce the anxiety that was interfering with his healing. He scheduled daily progressive relaxation sessions before and after every workout. Alan was also given a relaxation audiotape to listen to every night before he went to sleep. The relaxation exercises lowered his muscle tension, facilitating healing. They also made him feel more calm and in control, which bolstered his self-confidence. In general, he felt more comfortable, so he had a better attitude toward rehabilitation, was more motivated to train, and was able to concentrate during physical therapy sessions.

Dance Imagery for Injury Rehabilitation

As discussed, mental imagery is a powerful tool for improving physical, technical, and psychological performance. It can also be used to promote healing and maintain performance during rehabilitation.

Imagery may actually assist the healing process. Imagery has been used as part of the treatment of cancer and other illnesses (Achterberg, 1991; Hall, Rodgers & Barr, 1990; Simonton, Matthews-Simonton, & Creighton, 1978). It has also been shown to alter body temperature and increase blood flow.

For imagery to be used to facilitate injury recovery, injured dancers must have a full understanding of the damaged area and how the healing process works. Also, they should have a visual representation of the injured area. Having their physician or physical therapist give them a detailed description of the injury helps them develop an accurate image of the injured area. X-rays and diagrams are especially useful.

Injured dancers can then use the information described in chapter 5 to develop a dance imagery for injury rehabilitation program. Dancers should use imagery immediately following a relaxation session. Imagining the damaged area healing, for example, a broken bone mending or a torn ligament becoming whole.

Dance imagery during rehabilitation may also be used to maintain dance performance while dancers are unable to train. Unfortunate aspects of being injured are that dancers fall behind from where they were prior to injury and are unable to continue the progress in their dancing that would normally occur were they not injured.

But fortunately, dance imagery can be used to reduce the effects of lost training and performance time because it can produce skill and performance improvement without actual physical practice. Dance imagery also helps injured dancers psychologically and emotionally. Seeing themselves dancing regularly in their imagery results in greater self-confidence, a more positive attitude, and increased motivation. It gives them the sense that they are actively becoming a better dancer rather than falling behind their peers.

Dance imagery for injury rehabilitation can utilize the techniques described in chapter 5. Injured dancers should establish a program in which they alternate days of healing imagery with days of performance imagery. Most importantly, dance imagery should be structured as a regular and necessary part of dancers' rehabilitation programs.

Alan developed a two-part dance imagery program that focused on enhancing rehabilitation and maintaining dance skills. After getting a full description of his injured knee and how it heals, Alan engaged in healing imagery following the relaxation training session at the end of his daily rehabilitation workout. Also, three times a week, he followed his evening relaxation session with dance imagery. In these sessions, he would select, at first, specific skills performed in classes and imagine himself executing them. As his rehabilitation progressed, he chose particular roles and imagined himself performing in various productions.

Using PPEP Techniques in Rehabilitation

An important aspect of the rehabilitation process is how dancers respond to injury in terms of their thinking, emotions, and behavior. Injured dancers often overestimate the seriousness of the injury or become overly pessimistic about its consequences. Dancers may also experience significant grief over the loss of a valued activity. Furthermore, dancers may demonstrate self-defeating behavior, like returning to the stage before full recovery.

Due to unanticipated problems that may arise in the healing process, injured dancers should use the exercises described in the previous chapters to improve self-confidence, stay motivated, reduce anxiety, and maintain concentration, in addition to the techniques just discussed. Place particular emphasis on maintaining positive self-talk and emotions, alleviating fears about the quality of their recovery, and sustaining a high level of commitment to their rehabilitation program.

Alan chose several PPEP techniques to build his confidence, reduce his anxiety, and maintain his concentration. Specifically, he developed a dancer's litany that he repeated every morning and night, and used thought-stopping to control his negative thinking. He also practiced deep breathing when he became tense and smiled whenever he had negative thoughts. Alan developed some key words to use during his rehabilitation training to help him focus on each exercise, enabling him to put full effort and intensity into his workouts. He also kept a training diary to document his improvement.

Social Support

As mentioned, a lack of social support and feelings of loneliness and isolation make recovery particularly difficult. As a result, take active steps to ensure that your injured dancers maintain contact with other dancers and receive the support they need.

Teamwork.   One way to develop social support with injured dancers is to organize them into a training group of their own. This enables them to work together, support, and motivate each other. Have them create a special name for their group and design and wear a special "team uniform" t-shirt to give them the sense of being a part of something meaningful and reduce their feelings of isolation.

Support groups comprised of injured dancers or other performers such as athletes may also prove beneficial. These gatherings allow injured dancers to share their experiences of the rehabilitation process, discuss their progress, and express fears and worries they may have about their recovery or return to the stage.

Alan teamed up in his workouts with a professional baseball player, Ed, who was recovering from a similar injury. They encouraged each other and made sure they kept motivated. Alan also found that going to rehabilitation was no longer a chore for him. He was having fun and enjoyed talking to Ed about their injuries and their careers.

Group discussions with other performers.   Dancers' common reaction to injuries is feeling that they will never be able to recover fully and that their careers will be over. Due to the isolation that typically occurs, injured dancers often feel that they are the only ones who have ever felt this way. Counter these perceptions by having injured dancers meet periodically with other dancers who are recovering or have recovered successfully from serious injury. Group discussions enable injured dancers to see that their feelings are common and a normal reaction to the stress of an injury. Dancers also gain perspective and a sense of predictability from the now-healthy dancers describing what they went through and what the injured dancers can expect. Additionally, the meetings allow now-healthy dancers to offer practical ideas and tips to the injured dancers to facilitate their rehabilitation. Finally, they provide injured dancers with a positive role model, image, and attitude, and a sense of hope about their injury and the recovery that lies ahead.

The clinic in which Alan did his physical therapy offered weekly group meetings for recovering athletes and dancers. During these meetings, Alan found that other elite performers shared his concerns about recovery and returning to the performance arena. They also let him know what to expect in the later stages of rehabilitation and in his return to the studio. Alan experienced considerable relief and gained a more positive outlook about his recovery. You can organize similar meetings within your studio by using the recommendations made in this book.

Keep dancers involved.   When dancers become injured, they will often stop coming to the studio and lose contact with the other dancers. Take steps to keep injured dancers involved in the studio and its many activities. "Keeping injured dancers in their normal practice environment will minimize the psychosocial stresses that also occur following injury. We would like to avoid deconditioning not only physically . . . , but also in the psyche of the dancer" (Teitz, 1984, p. 81).

Though injured dancers may be unable to fully participate in classes, there may be some exercises you can adapt to work around their injury that they could do. For example, a dancer with an injured knee may not be able to do the leg movements in certain exercises, but could benefit from practicing the upper body and arm movements. Thus, the injured dancers maintain contact with the other dancers and also continue to improve some aspects of their dancing.

You may also include injured dancers in class time by having them assist you in organizing and teaching the class. They could, for example, announce each exercise. If they are experienced enough, they could help you make technical corrections. Naming them teacher's assistants or associate instructors would further enhance their feelings of involvement.

Injured dancers could be present and contributing during rehearsals and performances too. Giving them certain responsibilities, such as helping with costumes and makeup, cueing dancers on-stage, or directing dancers backstage, further maintains involvement and feelings that their careers are continuing despite the injury.

All of these experiences provide benefits beyond social support. Participating in different aspects of dance is educational and broadens appreciation for and understanding of the total dance experience. When dancers have recovered from injury they can use these experiences to enhance their performances and overall quality of their dance participation.

With encouragement from the dance mistress, Alan returned to the studio and participated in class as much as was possible with his injury. He found that he was able to work on technical areas, such as his arm position, which he never had time for previously. Alan also enjoyed being around his peers again. They were very supportive and looked forward to his return. Alan spoke to the director of the show in which he would have performed and was given the responsibility of organizing the dancers and preparing them for their cues during rehearsals and performances.

The culmination of this PReP was that Alan completed his rehabilitation on schedule. After a slow start, once these techniques were used, he was generally able to maintain a positive attitude and stay motivated to adhere to the program. Upon his return to the studio, he was surprised at how strong he was technically and physically, and how quickly he was able to reestablish his touch and artistry. Alan not only returned to his previous level of performance, but surpassed it and took on new and more demanding roles.

Mikko Nissinen, principal dancer for the San Francisco Ballet, on his own rehabilitation and return to the stage remarked:

> After eight months on the sidelines, an operation for a subsequent knee injury, and countless hours of grueling recuperative training. . . . Finally I am starting to feel that I am able to use my body again as a tool for art. This year I can feel the harmony in my body. I'm stronger from going through recovery, because of a fuller understanding of my own physique. (Gere, 1992, p. 32)

ENCORE

Many dancers will experience an injury at some time in their careers that will keep them out of the studio and off the stage. Surgical and rehabilitative techniques are so advanced that injured dancers can often expect a full physical recovery. Yet dancers do not always return to their preinjury level of performance.

This performance deficit may be due to psychological damage that occurred from the injury and the lack of rehabilitation of psychological factors that influence performance. Four psychological factors that will either facilitate or impede rehabilitation are self-confidence, motivation, anxiety, and concentration.

Self-confidence is important at three levels in the rehabilitation process: dancers must believe in the effectiveness of the rehabilitation program, that they will successfully complete the program, and that they will again perform at their preinjury level.

A high level of motivation is critical to endure the length, discomfort, and intensity of the rehabilitation process.

Anxiety hurts the recovery process by increasing pain, reducing self-confidence and motivation, and producing physical symptoms that inhibit healing.

During rehabilitation, effective concentration is necessary to maintain intensity and motivation, and during postrehabilitation, it is important to focus on performance rather than the injured area.

The Psychological Rehabilitation Program (PReP) is designed to optimize the four psychological factors and ensure a timely recovery. Five primary strategies compose a PReP: goal setting, relaxation training, dance imagery, social support, and PPEP techniques.

Goal setting provides injured dancers with increased commitment and motivation to the rehabilitation program, gives them a feeling of control, focuses injured dancers on the rehabilitation, and diverts attention away from negative aspects of the injury. Goals should be set for each phase of the rehabilitation process: physical, psychological, maintenance/return-to-form, and performance.

Relaxation training is aimed at reducing anxiety and lessening pain that will inhibit the healing process.

Dance imagery for injury rehabilitation may promote the healing process and minimize deterioration of performance-related skills.

The PReP focuses on the thinking, emotional, and behavioral responses to the injury. Emphasis is placed on improving self-confidence, staying motivated, reducing anxiety, and maintaining concentration.

Social support can be developed three ways to facilitate the recovery process: through support and teamwork among injured dancers, with group discussions with dancers who have recovered from injury, and by keeping injured dancers involved in the studio.

8

Developing a Psychological Program for Enhanced Performance (PPEP)

Dancing is a process, not a product. (Suzanne Farrell, 1990, p. 296)

Dress Rehearsal:
Designing and Implementing a Group PPEP

You are an instructor for a small but high-level youth ballet school and responsible for a group of gifted 11- to 14-year-old dancers. In 4 months, the school will be putting on their major production of the year, of which your group will assume the leading roles. For most of them, this will be their first starring opportunity.

1. What psychological issues are most likely to be evident in preparing for this production?
2. What techniques would you use to address these issues?
3. Design a group PPEP to meet the needs of your dancers preparing for the production.

The chapters thus far have introduced you to many techniques that may be used to enhance the performance of your dancers. However, it is not necessary for all of your dancers to use all of these techniques. Rather, individual dancers must select those strategies that will address their most immediate psychological needs. Before this can be done though, you must expose your dancers to these techniques, give them the opportunity to try them, and let the dancers decide which ones they prefer and are most effective.

A Psychological Program for Enhanced Performance (PPEP) may be likened to a road map. Just as a road map guides travelers to their destination, a PPEP directs dancers toward their destination of being mentally prepared to optimally perform. Also, just as how a person reads a map depends on who is doing the reading, so too must a PPEP be individualized to the dancer who will use it. Developing a PPEP that is appropriate for the level of dancers with whom you work involves three steps: designing a PPEP, implementing a PPEP, and maintaining a PPEP.

Center Stage:
Designing a Psychological Program
for Enhanced Performance (PPEP)

Have your dancers

• experiment with PPEP techniques described in the previous chapters,

- identify their individual psychological needs,
- specify PPEP techniques to be used to address their psychological needs,
- set PPEP goals for each area, and
- organize a daily and weekly schedule for implementing and maintaining PPEPs.

As instructor, strive to

- work with your dancers to identify group psychological needs,
- specify techniques and goals, and
- organize a schedule for implementing and maintaining group PPEPs.

DESIGNING A PPEP

When designing a PPEP, think back to the performing attitude pyramid discussed in the introduction. This pyramid includes all areas critical to a dancer's psychological preparation for performance: motivation, self-confidence, intensity, and concentration. An effective PPEP will take into account all of these areas. Within any dance group, whether a school or a company, two levels of needs should be considered. First, there are general psychological areas common to most, if not all, of your dancers that are in need of work. For example, most dancers could benefit from work on their self-confidence. Second, each of your dancers will have their own unique needs that must be addressed. Identifying needs at these two levels is the first step in designing group and individualized PPEPs.

Begin this PPEP development phase by prioritizing the psychological areas in need of work. For group PPEPs, draw on your experience with your dancers to determine the three most important areas on which you want to focus. For individualized PPEPs, use the performing attitude profiling described in Raising the Curtain on the Performing Attitude. The personal profile will assist you and your dancers in identifying their psychological areas in most immediate need of improvement and it may also be used as the basis for designing a PPEP. Drawing on the information obtained in the personal profile, have your dancers complete the PPEP Needs Identification form.

As you can see from the worksheet, dancers will have different psychological needs for the different settings in which they perform. For example, in the studio during class, a primary need might be to concentrate better on the exercises. During rehearsal, it might be to maintain confidence while learning a new and demanding role. On the night of a performance, a need could be to reduce intensity. Out of the studio, developing imagery skills may be the focus. Though it seems that there are many needs being ad-

PPEP Needs Identification

Directions: In the space below, indicate on the left side what you and your instructor believe are the psychological areas that need to be worked on in the different settings. Then on the right side, indicate the psychological techniques that you will use to develop the area. (Examples of psychological areas and techniques are given.)

Dance setting	Psychological area	Techniques
Studio	Concentration	Key words
1.		
2.		
3.		
Rehearsal	Confidence	Thought-stopping
1.		
2.		
3.		
Performance	Intensity	Progressive relaxation
1.		
2.		
3.		
Out-of-studio	Overall performance	Dance imagery
1.		
2.		
3.		

dressed, not all should necessarily be worked on at once. Instead, have your dancers address one or two until they have been developed, then have them move on to others.

This book has offered many psychological techniques to develop motivation, self-confidence, intensity, and concentration. (See Table 8.1 for an index of techniques discussed in this book.) It would not be necessary, however, for every dancer working on self-confidence to use every exercise we described. Though there is no firm rule of how many exercises should be used to work on a particular area, have your dancers select two or three that they prefer and incorporate them into their PPEP. Additionally, dance imagery should be a part of most dancers' PPEPs because it can be used to deal with almost every psychological need on which dancers are working.

While identifying techniques for the PPEP, assign specific goals for each area that will be addressed. The goal setting procedure described in chapter 1 can be used for this purpose. Dancers should follow the guidelines offered there in establishing motivating objectives for all of their psychological needs.

Once the dancers have identified their psychological needs, indicated what exercises they will use, and set specific goals for each of these areas,

Table 8.1 Psychological Program for Enhanced Performance Index

Psychological need	Chapter	PPEP technique	Page
Motivation	1	Goal setting Training partner Motivational cues Daily questions	19
Self-confidence	2	Preparation Role models Walk the walk Dancer's litany Thought-stopping	37
Intensity	3	Breathing Progressive relaxation Preperformance routines High energy thinking and imagery	49
Concentration	4	Key words Dance imagery Backstage management	69
Dance imagery	5	Developing a dance imagery program	85

they can then organize this information into a structured PPEP. Table 8.2 illustrates a daily PPEP plan that incorporates self-confidence and intensity exercises into a cohesive program. You may also develop a group PPEP for class and rehearsal.

In developing an effective PPEP, your dancers have to ask the following questions:

(a) How motivated am I to adhere to a PPEP? and

(b) How much time can I devote to the PPEP, both in and out of the studio?

With these questions answered, your dancers can take the needs, techniques, and goals, and organize them into a structured daily and weekly routine with the use of the PPEP Planner. As demonstrated in the PPEP Planner worksheet, your dancers specify the day and time that they will use a particular technique. For example, as shown in the planner, a dancer has written "7 a.m., say litany" in the morning box. She will refer to her planner to see what her PPEP responsibilities are each day.

Use a similar process to organize a group PPEP, in which you identify common needs, techniques, and goals that you can incorporate into class and rehearsal time. Table 8.3 illustrates a group PPEP. It is likely that your group PPEP and your dancers' individualized PPEPs will overlap somewhat. This common ground will not only make it easier for your dancers to adhere to their program in class and rehearsal, but it will also support and encourage their efforts outside of the studio.

Table 8.2   Sample PPEP

7:00 a.m.—Wake-up: say dancer's litany out loud.

12:00 p.m.—Lunch: set daily training goals.

12:30 p.m.—Leave for training: walk the walk, talk the talk.

1:00 p.m.—Training: incorporate PPEP skills into class.

- Dance imagery
- Key words
- Pre-exercise routines
- Relaxation techniques
- Self-confidence techniques

6:00 p.m.—Do relaxation exercises and dance imagery.

10:00 p.m.—Update daily training journal.

11:00 p.m.—Bedtime: say dancer's litany out loud.

PPEP Planner

Time	Example	Monday	Tuesday	Wednesday	Thursday	Friday	Saturday	Sunday
M O R N I N G	*7:00 a.m.* say litany							
A F T E R N O O N	*12:00 noon* set goals *12:30 p.m.* walk the walk *1:00 p.m.* use PPEP technique in class							
E V E N I N G	*6:00 p.m.* relaxation exercises, imagery *10:00 p.m.* update journal *11:00 p.m.* say litany							

Table 8.3   Example of Group PPEP

Psychological need and goal	Technique	Time
Increase motivation	Goal setting	At start of off-season; monthly meetings with dancers
	Two daily questions	At start and end of class
Build self-confidence	Dancer's litany	At start and end of class and rehearsal
	Walk the walk, talk the talk	Anytime in class
Intensity control	Breathing	Before every exercise
	Progressive relaxation	At end of class
	Preperformance routines	Before every role rehearsal
Overall performance	Dance imagery	Three times per week

This first step in developing a PPEP is the most time-consuming because it involves learning the many techniques that are available and trying them out to see what works best. Also, it requires that your dancers take the time to design a PPEP, evaluating, planning, and organizing each aspect. This step requires a commitment of several hours per week out of the studio in addition to time devoted to trying the techniques during class and rehearsal, and can last one to two months.

IMPLEMENTING A PPEP

One misconception held by many dancers is that psychological skills training can produce fast, often miraculous results. Starting to use these skills two days before a performance won't help. Though sometimes immediate results do occur, more realistically, the development of psychological skills, just like physical and technical skills, takes time and practice. PPEPs should not be begun near to or during the performance season. This time of year is busy and stressful enough without introducing a new and different component to a dancer's life and training program. This also ensures that dancers will not have unrealistic expectations about the PPEP and be looking for a quick fix to their performance problems.

Consequently, dancers should begin implementing PPEPs several months before the performance season begins. Starting a PPEP early in the year has several benefits. It gives dancers the opportunity to develop an effective program. It allows them to slowly incorporate it into their dance training regimen. It enables them to fine-tune the program to best suit their needs. Finally, it affords them the time to practice the skills and obtain benefits. This second step of implementing a PPEP involves your dancers consistently adhering to it, engaging in the techniques and exercises, and developing the psychological skills addressed in the program. This step should begin at least three months prior to the start of the performance season and continue to its conclusion. It requires 10 to 15 minutes, four times per week, away from the studio, incorporating selected techniques into class and rehearsal, and will last from 6 to 12 months.

Maintaining a PPEP

How long should dancers use the PPEP? There is really no end to the use of psychological skills training. Just like physical and technical skills, psychological skills will atrophy when not maintained through practice. Legs don't get stronger if they are only exercised once a week, and technique doesn't improve if it is only practiced once a week. The same is true of psychological skills. Earlier we discussed the positive change formula: awareness + control + repetition = positive change. It is in the implementation and maintenance phases of the PPEP that an understanding of the positive change formula becomes especially important. A critical part of using a PPEP is the commitment on the part of you and your dancers to maintain it consistently. As with any type of learning, repetition, the third element of the positive change formula, is essential for developing the performing attitude and meaningful, long-lasting psychological improvement in your dancers. One benefit of the regular use of a PPEP is that, with practice, the skills become more automatic, so less time and effort have to be spent on them. Once a sound level of psychological strength has been reached, all that is required is maintenance, which is less time- and energy-intensive.

In this final phase, dancers have established a solid foundation of psychological skills that enable them to perform at a consistently high level. As a result, dancers can modify their PPEPs to require a lower, though still consistent, level of commitment. Additionally, as specific problems arise, particular PPEP techniques can be added to resolve those difficulties. PPEP maintenance requires less time during class and rehearsal, and perhaps 5 to 10 minutes a day, two days per week.

ENCORE

Developing a Psychological Program for Enhanced Performance (PPEP) involves three steps: designing a PPEP, implementing a PPEP, and maintaining a PPEP

Designing PPEPs involves identifying the individual and group psychological needs of your dancers, specifying which PPEP techniques to use to address those needs, setting goals for each area, and organizing this information into a structured schedule.

Implementing a PPEP should begin several months before the performance season to give dancers time to develop an effective program, enable them to fine-tune the program to best suit their needs, and afford them the time to practice the skills and obtain benefits.

Implementation requires 10 to 15 minutes, four times per week, away from the studio, incorporating selected techniques into class and rehearsal, and will last from 6 to 12 months.

Long-term maintenance of a PPEP is important to keep a high level of psychological strength and to prevent your dancers' psychological skills from atrophying.

Dancers can modify their PPEPs in the maintenance stage to require a lower, though still consistent, level of commitment. Also, as specific problems occur, they can be addressed and alleviated quickly.

References

Achterberg, J. (1991, May). *Enhancing the immune function through imagery.* Paper presented at the Fourth World Conference on Imagery, Minneapolis.

Astaire, F. (1984). *The dancer's notebook.* Philadelphia: Running Press.

Bandura, A. (1977). Self-efficacy: Toward a unifying theory of behavioral change. *Psychological Review, 84*, 91-215.

Banes, S. (1980). *Terpsichore in sneakers: Post-modern dance.* Boston: Houghton Mifflin.

Boutcher, S.H., & Crews, D.J. (1987). The effect of a preshot attentional routine on a well-learned skill. *International Journal of Sport Psychology, 18*, 30-39.

Bunker, L., & Williams, J.M. (1986). Cognitive techniques for improving performance and building confidence. In J.M. Williams (Ed.), *Applied sport psychology: Personal growth to peak performance* (pp. 235-255). Palo Alto, CA: Mayfield.

Bursill, A.E. (1958). Restriction of peripheral vision during exposure to hot and humid conditions. *Quarterly Journal of Experimental Psychology, 10*, 113-119.

Butler, R.J. (1989). Psychological preparation of Olympic boxers. In J. Kremer & W. Crawford (Eds.), *The psychology of sport: Theory and practice* (pp. 74-84). Leicester, England: British Psychological Society.

Carron, A.V. (1984). *Motivation: Implications for coaching and teaching.* London, Ontario: Sports Dynamics.

Cautela, J.R., & Wisocki, P.A. (1977). Thought-stoppage procedure: Description, application, and learning theory interpretations. *Psychological Record, 27*, 255-264.

Clark, L. (1960). Effect of mental practice on the development of a certain motor skill. *Research Quarterly, 31*, 560-569.

Cohn, P.J., Rotella, R.J., & Lloyd, J.W. (1990). Effects of a cognitive behavioral intervention on the preshot routine and performance in golf. *The Sport Psychologist, 4*, 33-47.

Csikszentmihalyi, M. (1975). *Beyond boredom and anxiety.* San Francisco: Jossey-Bass.

Cunningham, M. (1951). The function of a technique for dance. In W. Sorell (Ed.), *The dance has many faces* (pp. 250-251). New York: World Publishing.

Danish, S.J. (1986). Psychological aspects in the care and treatment of athletic injuries. In P.E. Vinger, & E.F. Hoerner (Eds.), *Sports injuries: The unthwarted epidemic* (pp. 345-353). Littleton, MA: PSG.

deMille, A. (1952). *Dance with the piper.* New York: Bantam.

deMille, R. (1981). *Put your mother on the ceiling.* Santa Barbara: Ross-Erickson.

Doob, P. (1982). Jennifer Penney: Modest reflections on the road to stardom. *Dance in Canada Danse ou,* **32**, 10-12.

Dowd, I. (1981). *Taking root to fly: Seven articles on functional anatomy.* New York: I. Dowd.

Duda, J. L., Smart, A.E. , & Tappe, M.K. (1989). Predictors of adherence in the rehabilitation of physical injuries: An application of personal investment theory. *Journal of Sport and Exercise Psychology,* **11**, 367-381.

Duncan, I. (1974). The dance of the future. In S.J. Cohen (Ed.), *Dance as a theatre art: Source readings in dance history from 1581 to the present* (pp. 123-129). New York: Dodd, Mead.

Ellfeldt, L. (1976). *Dance: From magic to art.* Dubuque, IA: William C. Brown.

Feltz, D.L., & Landers, D.M. (1983). The effects of mental practice on motor skill learning and performance: A meta-analysis. *Journal of Sport Psychology,* **5**, 25-57.

Flatow, S. (1982). Starting over. *Ballet News,* **6**, 16-18, 40.

Gelatt, R. (1980), *Nijinsky: The film.* New York: Ballantine.

Gere, D. (1992, August). Mikko Nissinen: Strength regained, confidence restored. *Dance,* **8**, 32-37.

Gould, D. (1986). Goal setting for peak performance. In J.M. Williams (Ed.), *Applied sport psychology: Personal growth to peak performance* (pp. 133-148). Palo Alto, CA: Mayfield.

Gould, D., Horn, T., & Spreemann, J. (1983). Sources of stress in junior elite wrestlers. *Journal of Sport Psychology,* **5**, 159-171.

Graham, M. (1974). A modern dancer's primer for action. In S.J. Cohen (Ed.), *Dance as a theatre art: Source readings in dance history from 1581 to the present* (pp. 135-142). New York: Dodd, Mead, & Company.

Greenhill, J. (1992). A critical step toward a ballet career. *Dance Teacher Now,* **14**, 53-58.

Greenspan, M.J., & Feltz, D.L. (1989). Psychological interventions with athletes in competitive situations: A review. *The Sport Psychologist,* **3**, 219-236.

Hanrahan, C., & Salmela, J.H. (1990). Dance images: Do they really work or are we just imagining things? *Journal of Physical Education, Recreation, and Dance,* **61**, 18-21.

Hardy, C.J., & Crace, R.K. (1990, May/June). Dealing with injury. *Sport Psychology Training Bulletin,* **1**, 1-8.

Harris, D.V. (1986). Relaxation and energizing techniques for regulation of arousal. In J.M. Williams (Ed.), *Applied sport psychology: Personal growth to peak performance* (pp. 185-207). Palo Alto, CA: Mayfield.

H'Doubler, M.N. (1968). *Dance: A creative art experience.* Madison, WI: The University of Wisconsin Press.

Helin, P. (1987). Mental and psychophysiological tension at professional ballet dancers' performances and rehearsals. *Dance Teacher Now, 21*, 7-14.

Henschen, K.P. (1993). Athletic staleness and burnout: Diagnosis, prevention, and treatment. In J.M. Williams (Ed.), *Applied sport psychology: Personal growth to peak performance* (pp. 328-337). Palo Alto, CA: Mayfield.

Heyman, S.R. (1984). Cognitive interventions: Theories, applications, and cautions. In W.F. Straub, & J.M. Williams (Eds.), *Cognitive sport psychology* (pp. 289-303). Lansing, NY: Sport Science Associates.

Holm, H. (1979). "Hanya speaks." In J.M. Brown (Ed.), *The vision of modern dance* (pp. 71-82). Princeton, NJ: Princeton Book.

Humphrey, D. (1951). *The art of making dances.* New York: Grove Press.

Hunt, M. (1992, April). Return of the prodigal mentor: Benjamin Harkarvy. *Dance, 4*, 52-56.

Ievleva, L., & Orlick, T. (1991). Mental links to enhanced healing: An exploratory study. *The Sport Psychologist, 5*, 25-40.

Jacobson, E. (1938). *Progressive relaxation.* Chicago: University of Chicago Press.

Kreemer, C. (1987). *Further steps: Fifteen choreographers on modern dance.* New York: Harper & Row.

Landers, D.M. (1978). Motivation and performance: The role of arousal and attentional factors. In W.F. Straub (Ed.), *Sport psychology: An analysis of athlete behavior* (pp. 91-103). Ithaca, NY: Mouvement.

Landers, D.M., & Boutcher, S.H. (1986). Arousal-performance relationships. In J.M. Williams (Ed.), *Applied sport psychology: Personal growth to peak performance* (pp. 163-184). Palo Alto, CA: Mayfield.

Leith, G. (1972). The relationship between intelligence, personality, and creativity under two conditions of stress. *British Journal of Educational Psychology, 42*, 240-247.

Locke, E.A., & Latham, G.P. (1985). The applications of goal setting to sports. *Journal of Sport Psychology, 7*, 205-222.

Loren, T. (1978). *The dancer's companion: The indispensable guide to getting the most out of dance classes.* New York: The Dial Press.

Louis, M. (1977, February). From the inside: On teachers. *Dance Magazine.* p. 84.

Lyle, C. (1977). *Dancers on dancing.* New York: Drake.

Manley, M., & Wilson, V.E. (1980). Anxiety, creativity, and dance performance. *Dance Research Journal, 12*, 11-22.

Martens, R., Burton, D., Vealey, R., Bump, L., & Smith, D. (1983). *The development of the Competitive State Anxiety Inventory-2* (CA\SAI-2). Unpublished manuscript.

Meek, L. (1992). Profile of a dancer. *Journal of Physical Education, Recreation, and Dance, 38*.

Montee, K. (1992). Miami City Ballet: Moving fast. *Dance, 10*, 43-45.

Moore, W.E., & Stevenson, J.R. (1991). Understanding trust in the perform-ance of complex automatic sport skills. *The Sport Psychologist*, **5**, 281-289.

Newman, B. (1982). *Striking a balance: Dancers talk about dancing*. Boston: Houghton Mifflin.

Nideffer, R.M. (1976). Test of attentional and interpersonal style. *Journal of Personality and Social Psychology*, **34**, 394-404.

Nideffer, R.M. (1986). Concentration and attentional control training. In J.M. Williams (Ed.), *Applied sport psychology: Personal growth to peak perform-ance* (pp. 257-269). Palo Alto, CA: Mayfield.

Noverre, G. (1974). Two letters on dancing. In S. J. Cohen (Ed.), *Dance as a theatre art: Source readings in dance history from 1581 to the present* (pp. 57-64). New York: Dodd, Mead.

Oxendine, J.B. (1970). Emotional arousal and motor performance. *Quest*, **13**, 23-32.

Penrod, J., & Plastino, J.G. (1980). *The dancer prepares: Modern dance for beginners*. Palo Alto, CA: Mayfield.

Rick, C. (1971/1972). A dancer's thoughts: Seduction. *DanceScope*, **6**, 54-55.

Rosen, L.F. (1977). Talking with Agnes deMille. *DanceScope*, **11**, 8-17.

Rotella, R.J., & Heyman, S.R. (1993). Stress, injury, and the psychological rehabilitation of athletes. In J.M. Williams (Ed.), *Applied sport psychology: Personal growth to peak performance* (pp. 338-355). Palo Alto, CA: May-field.

Rushall, B.S. (1986). The content of competition thinking. In W.F. Straub & J.M. Williams (Eds.), *Cognitive sport psychology* (pp. 51-62). Lansing, NY: Sport Science Associates.

Sande, R. (1977). The experience of dance theatre. In J. Schlaich & B. DuPont (Eds.), *Dance: The art of production* (pp. 1-8). St. Louis: Mosby.

Sarno, J. (1984). *Mind over back pain*. New York: Morrow & Co.

Schmid, A., & Peper, E. (1986). Techniques for training concentration. In J.M. Williams (Ed.), *Applied sport psychology: Personal growth to peak perform-ance* (pp. 271-284). Palo Alto, CA: Mayfield.

Schnitt, D. (1990). Psychological issues in dancers—An overview. *Journal of Physical Education, Recreation, and Dance*, 32-34.

Sheets, M. (1966). *The phenomenology of dance*. Madison, WI: The University of Wisconsin Press.

Silva, J.M., & Hardy, C.J. (1984). Precompetitive affect and athletic perform-ance. In W. F. Straub & J.M. Williams (Eds.), *Cognitive sport psychology* (pp. 79-88). Lansing, NY: Sport Science Associates.

Simonton, O.C., Matthews-Simonton, S., & Creighton, J.L. (1978). *Getting well again*. New York: Bantam.

Smith, D. (1987). Conditions that facilitate the development of sport imagery training. *The Sport Psychologist*, **1**, 237-247.

Smith, K.L. (1990). Dance and imagery: The link between movement and imagination. *Journal of Physical Education, Recreation, and Dance*, **61**, 17.

Sorell, W. (1971). *The dancer's image: Points and counterpoints.* New York: Columbia University.

Stodelle, E. (1984). *Deep song: The Dance Story of Martha Graham.* New York: Schirmer.

Taylor, J. (1988). Psychological aspects of teaching and coaching tennis. In J.L. Groppel (Ed.), *The USPTA sport science and sports medicine guide* (pp. 133-147). Wesley Chapel, FL: USPTA.

Taylor, J. (1988). Slumpbusting: A systematic analysis of slumps in sports. *The Sport Psychologist, 2,* 39-48.

Taylor, J. (1991). *The mental edge for competitive sports.* Denver, CO: Minuteman Press.

Taylor, J., & Taylor, C. (1987, January/February). The mental attitude: Self-confidence. *Dance Teacher Now,* 16-17.

Taylor, J., & Taylor, C. (1987, June). Mental attitude: Motivation. *Dance Teacher Now,* 10-11.

Taylor, J., & Taylor, C. (1987, September). Mental attitude: Goal setting. *Dance Teacher Now,* 8-10.

Tharp, T. (1992). *Push comes to shove.* New York: Bantam.

Wallach, M.A., & Kogan, N. (1965). A new look at the creativity-intelligence distinction. In P. Vernon (Ed.), *Creativity* (pp. 235-256). Baltimore: Penguin Education.

Williams, J.M., & Roepke, N. (1993). Psychology of injury and injury rehabilitation. In R.N. Singer, M. Murphey, & L.K. Tennant (Eds.), *Handbook on research on sport psychology* (pp. 815-839). New York: Macmillan.

Woolfolk, R. L., Murphy, S. M., Gottesfeld, D., & Aitken, D. (1985). Effects of mental rehearsal of task motor activity and mental depiction of task outcome on motor skill performance. *Journal of Sport Psychology, 7,* 191-197.

Yerkes, R.M., & Dodson, J.D. (1908). The relation of strength of stimulus to rapidity of habit formation. *Journal of Comparative Neurology of Psychology, 18,* 459-482.

Zajonc, R.B. (1985). Emotion and facial efference: A theory reclaimed. *Science, 228,* 15-21.

Index

About the Authors

Jim Taylor, PhD, is a psychologist recognized for his work in the psychological aspects of performance in sport and the performing arts. He has implemented a psychological services program for the Miami City Ballet, lectured at the Hartford Ballet Company, and served as a consultant and member of the faculty at the DanceAspen Summer School. A former associate professor at Nova University in Ft. Lauderdale, Dr. Taylor has published more than 140 scholarly and popular articles, including a series of articles in *Dance Teacher Now*, and presented more than 150 workshops internationally. Jim is a former dancer and world-ranked Alpine ski racer and holds a second-degree black belt in karate.

Ceci Taylor's 40 years of experience as a professional dancer, professor of dance, and dance counselor have given her unique insight into the psychological demands of dance. With master's degrees in both dance and counseling, she has used her rich background to lecture and write about the psychological issues of dance, including coauthoring a column in *Dance Teacher Now*. A professor emeritus at St. Joseph College (Hartford, CT) and counselor to the Hartford Ballet, Ceci hopes this book will inspire other instructors to recognize the need to address the spirit as well as the body of the dancer.

Related books from Human Kinetics

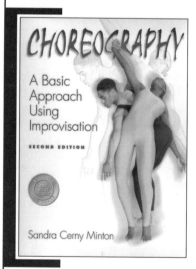